Copyright © 2024 Andrea Oliver

All rights reserved

The characters and events portrayed in this book are fictitious. Any similarity to real persons, living or dead, is coincidental and not intended by the author.

No part of this book may be reproduced, or stored in a retrieval system, or transmitted in any form or by any means, electronic, mechanical, photocopying, recording, or otherwise, without express written permission of the publisher.

Cover design by: Art Painter
Library of Congress Control Number: 2018675309
Printed in the United States of America

CONTENTS

Copyright

Introduction   2

Chapter 1: Introduction to the E-2 Visa   5

Chapter 2: Setting Personal and Financial Expectations   13

Chapter 3: Choosing the Right Business Model for E-2 Investment   23

Chapter 4: Forming Partnerships, Joint Ventures, and Alternative Structures   32

Chapter 5: Crafting a Winning Business Plan   41

Chapter 6: Compiling Required Documentation   51

Chapter 7: Preparing for and Navigating the E-2 Visa Interview   60

Chapter 8: Legal and Compliance Requirements Post-Approval   68

Chapter 9: Setting Up Your Business Operations in the U.S.   77

Chapter 10: Marketing and Expanding Your E-2 Business   87

Chapter 11: Preparing for E-2 Visa Renewal   96

Chapter 12: Long-Term Strategies and Alternative Residency Options   104

Chapter 13: Common Pitfalls and How to Avoid Them   113

Chapter 14: Success Stories and Case Studies   121

Appendices   129

ANDREAOLIVER

The Ultimate Guide to Becoming an E-2 Investor:

Pathway to U.S. Business Residency

INTRODUCTION

The allure of living and working in the United States is undeniable for many investors, entrepreneurs, and business-minded individuals around the world. The E-2 investor visa offers a unique and accessible path to U.S. residency through investment in a business venture—whether it's starting a new company, purchasing an existing business, or diving into the world of franchising. However, navigating the E-2 process can feel overwhelming, especially when facing the intricate regulations, strategic choices, and financial requirements needed to achieve success.

This guide is designed to provide you with a practical, straightforward approach to becoming an E-2 investor, taking you from concept to U.S. residency with detailed, step-by-step guidance. In these pages, you will discover everything you need to make informed decisions, structure a compliant and profitable business, and confidently move through the visa application process. From choosing the right business model and understanding necessary legal structures to preparing for the all-important consulate interview, this book is a resource crafted to demystify each stage of the E-2 journey.

In addition to the technical insights, this guide includes real-world tips, examples, and practical advice tailored to meet the needs of prospective E-2 investors with diverse backgrounds, capital, and business goals. We'll explore alternative pathways, options for partnerships, and long-term planning strategies so you can approach the E-2 process with a sense of clarity, purpose, and optimism.

If you're ready to take the first step toward building a business in the U.S., this guide will give you the roadmap you need. Let's get started.

Part 1: Understanding the E-2 Visa Framework

CHAPTER 1: INTRODUCTION TO THE E-2 VISA

Imagine being able to move to the United States, start a business, live with your family, and take advantage of everything the country has to offer—all without needing family ties, a job offer, or even a college degree. For many people, that sounds too good to be true. But for those willing to invest in a U.S.-based business, the E-2 visa makes this possible. It's a unique visa that centers around entrepreneurship and economic growth, allowing investors to build and manage businesses in the U.S. while experiencing the benefits of living there.

In this chapter, we'll introduce the E-2 visa, tracing its history and purpose. We'll cover what it takes to qualify, including eligibility requirements and investment basics. We'll also look at the benefits and limitations, so you'll know what to expect. Finally, we'll give a high-level overview of the E-2 application process. Whether you're interested in starting a business from scratch, buying an existing one, or joining a joint venture, this chapter sets the stage for understanding what the E-2 visa offers and what it takes to get there.

E-2 Visa: Definition, History, and Purpose

The E-2 visa is designed specifically for investors—foreign nationals who are willing to make a substantial financial commitment to a business in the United States. Unlike other visas tied to employment, family, or student status, the E-2 visa focuses on creating jobs and stimulating economic growth. This visa allows foreign investors to not only live in the U.S. but also build businesses that contribute to the American economy.

The E-2 visa has its roots in treaties established as early as the 1920s, when the U.S. began creating agreements with other countries to encourage mutual investment. These treaties were part of a broader movement to foster international economic cooperation, and the idea was simple: by promoting cross-border business, both the U.S. and the treaty countries would benefit. The E-2 visa made it possible for citizens of these countries to invest in the U.S., start businesses, and create jobs, thereby stimulating economic growth on both sides.

Today, the E-2 visa still holds true to this original purpose. It's a pathway for citizens of treaty countries to enter the U.S. through investment, fostering a spirit of international entrepreneurship. E-2 investors come from all over the world—Japan, Italy, Australia, and many other countries—with dreams of building businesses that not only generate profit but also contribute to local communities.

Anecdote: How an Entrepreneur Used the E-2 to Start a Boutique Hotel

I once met an entrepreneur from Argentina who used the E-2 visa to start a boutique hotel in Southern California. She had always dreamed of creating a space that combined sustainable design with luxury, and the E-2 visa offered her a way to turn that vision into reality in the U.S. By investing in the property, hiring a small team, and actively managing the business, she didn't just secure a visa; she built a thriving business that attracts eco-conscious travelers from around the world.

Eligibility Requirements: Treaty Countries, Who Qualifies, and

Basics on Required Investment

The E-2 visa offers an incredible opportunity, but like any immigration pathway, it has specific eligibility requirements. Here's a breakdown of the key factors that determine eligibility: nationality, investment size, and management role.

1. Treaty Country Requirement

To qualify for an E-2 visa, you must be a citizen of a country that has an E-2 treaty with the United States. These treaties exist with a wide range of countries—from major economic players like Germany and Japan to smaller nations like Grenada and Jordan. A full list of these countries is available in the appendix, and eligibility hinges on the passport you use to apply. For dual citizens, this means you'll need to apply with a passport from an eligible treaty country.

Anecdote: How Dual Citizenship Expanded One Entrepreneur's Options

One entrepreneur I met held dual citizenship with Mexico and Spain. While Spain doesn't have an E-2 treaty with the U.S., Mexico does. This meant he could apply through his Mexican nationality, allowing him to start a tech consulting firm in Miami. For him, dual citizenship opened doors that otherwise wouldn't have been accessible, illustrating how nationality can directly impact E-2 eligibility.

Tip: If you have dual citizenship, check to see if either of your countries has an E-2 treaty with the U.S. That passport might be your key to unlocking this visa pathway.

2. Investment Requirements

The E-2 visa requires what's called a "substantial" investment. While the term is open to interpretation, it generally means an amount significant enough to show that the investor is committed to making the business succeed. Importantly, there's no specific minimum dollar amount; the required investment depends on the business type and scale. A tech company may need a larger investment than a small retail store, for example.

A crucial point to understand is that the investment needs to be "at risk," meaning it's already committed to the business and has the potential for loss if the business doesn't succeed. The funds should be actively invested in areas essential for starting or running the business, such as purchasing equipment, securing a lease, or paying for necessary permits.

Case Study: What Constitutes a Substantial Investment?

A European investor I know started a small bakery in Seattle. She invested about $100,000 to cover equipment, the lease, and initial operating costs. This amount was sufficient to show her commitment to making the business viable without needing an extraordinary sum. In her case, the investment reflected the financial needs of the business, making it a qualifying amount under the E-2 guidelines.

Tip: When planning your investment, consider what it will realistically take to get your business off the ground. Substantial doesn't mean millions; it means enough to demonstrate your dedication and ensure the business's viability.

3. Active Management Requirement

The E-2 visa isn't designed for passive investors; it's for those who are actively involved in the business. E-2 visa holders must take on a managerial role, making day-to-day decisions and guiding the business's growth. This active management component is essential, as the E-2 visa aims to attract investors who are directly contributing to the business's success.

Example: Managing a Business with the E-2

A British investor I know opened a wellness studio in Los Angeles. She didn't just fund the business; she was involved in every aspect of operations, from hiring instructors to planning the studio's growth strategy. Her active role demonstrated that she was more than a financial backer—she was essential to the business's success. This hands-on involvement met the E-2's active management requirement, securing her visa status.

Tip: Be prepared to show that you're actively involved. Keep records of your responsibilities, business plans, and strategic decisions to demonstrate your commitment to the business's success.

Advantages and Limitations: Residency Benefits, Employment Flexibility, and Pathways Beyond E-2

The E-2 visa offers several benefits, but it also has limitations that investors need to consider. Here's an overview of the main advantages and some potential drawbacks.

1. Residency Benefits for the Investor and Family

E-2 visa holders and their immediate family members (spouse and children under 21) can live in the U.S. as long as the visa is valid. This visa is generally issued in increments of two to five years, and it can be renewed indefinitely, provided the business remains active and profitable. For families, this means access to U.S. education and healthcare and the ability to immerse themselves in the American lifestyle.

Anecdote: Family Life on an E-2 Visa

I once met an entrepreneur from South Korea who moved to the U.S. with his family on an E-2 visa to start a Korean-style fried chicken restaurant. While he managed the restaurant, his children attended local schools and his spouse found work in the local community. The family became active members of their neighborhood, blending their heritage with American culture, all thanks to the flexibility of the E-2 visa.

2. Employment Flexibility for Spouses

A unique benefit of the E-2 visa is the work flexibility it provides to spouses. While the investor must stay committed to managing their business, the spouse can apply for a work permit, allowing them to work in any field or even start their own business. This flexibility isn't common with other visa types and can be especially helpful for dual-income families.

Example: E-2 Spouse Starting Their Own Business

A German E-2 visa holder who opened a furniture design company in Texas had a spouse who used the work permit to start her own small café nearby. The café complemented the furniture business, creating a local connection that enhanced both ventures. This employment flexibility was key to the family's financial stability and local engagement.

3. Limitations: No Direct Path to Permanent Residency and Visa Dependency

The E-2 visa has its limitations, particularly in terms of long-term residency. The E-2 doesn't provide a direct pathway to a green card or U.S. citizenship. Many E-2 investors who wish to stay in the U.S. long-term eventually explore other options, such as the EB-5 investor visa or an employment-based green card.

Additionally, the E-2 visa is directly tied to the business's performance. If the business struggles or if the investor is no longer actively involved, the visa status may be at risk. This dependency requires careful business planning and financial stability.

Tip: For long-term residency, consider complementary visa options. Many E-2 visa holders explore options like the EB-5 or employment-based visas to eventually secure permanent residency.

Overview of the E-2 Process: High-Level Steps for the E-2 Process to Set the Stage for the Guide

Navigating the E-2 process may seem complex, but breaking it down into manageable steps can make the journey more straightforward. Here's a high-level overview of the E-2 process:

1. Research and Planning

Start by confirming your eligibility based on nationality, understanding the requirements for substantial investment, and identifying a business that aligns with E-2 criteria.

2. Securing an Investment

Decide whether you want to start a new business, buy an existing one, or join a partnership. Ensure that your investment meets the substantial criteria and reflects a real commitment to business success.

3. Preparing a Business Plan

The business plan is essential. This document should detail the business's financial projections, job creation plans, and operational strategies. U.S. Citizenship and Immigration Services (USCIS) uses this to assess the viability and impact of your investment.

4. Compiling Documentation

Gather all necessary documentation, including proof of nationality, investment source, business ownership, and any required licenses or agreements. This paperwork is crucial for demonstrating eligibility.

5. Submitting the Application

Apply for the E-2 visa through a U.S. consulate in your home country or from within the U.S. if eligible. This step involves fees, application forms, and submission of your business plan and supporting documents.

6. Attending the Visa Interview

Prepare for an interview where you'll discuss your business plan, investment, and role in the business. This is your chance to show your commitment and capability as an investor.

7. Establishing and Running Your Business

Once approved, you can enter the U.S. and start managing your business. Remember, the E-2 visa requires active management to maintain compliance.

8. Preparing for Renewal or Exit Strategy

E-2 visas are renewable indefinitely as long as the business remains active. However, long-term planning may involve exploring options for permanent residency or an eventual exit strategy.

CHAPTER 2: SETTING PERSONAL AND FINANCIAL EXPECTATIONS

Starting a new life in a different country is exciting, and the E-2 visa offers an incredible opportunity to make that dream a reality through entrepreneurship. However, jumping into an investment that affects your financial stability, family life, and long-term plans isn't something to take lightly. This chapter is about laying the groundwork for success by helping you set realistic expectations and make informed financial decisions. From preparing the necessary funds to evaluating risk, we'll cover everything you need to set yourself up for success.

Investing in a U.S.-based business is about more than just financial preparation; it's about understanding your personal goals, the lifestyle changes that come with moving to a new country, and how your investment will impact your family's future. Let's dive into what it takes to prepare for this journey financially and personally.

Personal Financial Preparation: Gathering Capital, Documenting the Source of Funds, and Proving Legitimate Financial Sources

One of the most crucial steps in applying for an E-2 visa is securing and documenting the funds you'll use for your investment. This doesn't just mean having enough capital—it means being able to show where that money came from and proving it's legitimate. U.S. immigration authorities take these requirements seriously, and thorough preparation can save you a lot of headaches later on.

1. Gathering Capital

First things first: you'll need to gather the necessary funds to cover your investment. How much capital you need depends on the business you're investing in, but a common range is between $100,000 and $300,000. For some businesses, especially smaller ones, the amount may be lower, but it still has to be enough to be considered "substantial" for the business's operations.

Anecdote: How One Investor Built Her Capital Over Time

I once met an investor from the Netherlands who had her heart set on starting a café in San Francisco. She didn't have all the funds right away, so she took on freelance work, saved for years, and carefully budgeted until she had enough to make a substantial investment. Her journey shows that while it's challenging, gathering capital for an E-2 investment is possible with determination and planning.

Tip: Take a realistic look at your savings, potential funding sources, and any liquid assets. For most people, the investment isn't something they can pull together overnight, so start planning well in advance to build your capital.

2. Documenting the Source of Funds

Once you have your capital, documenting the source of these funds is essential. Immigration officials want to ensure the investment money wasn't obtained through illegal means or sketchy channels, so they'll require a paper trail. This means gathering evidence that shows the origin of your funds, whether they came from savings, property sales, loans, or gifts.

Example: Acceptable Documentation Sources

Let's say you received a large portion of your capital from selling a property. In this case, you'd need to provide proof of the sale, such as a sales contract, property title transfer, and bank statements showing the funds were deposited into your account. If part of your investment comes from a family gift, you'll need a formal gift letter stating the amount and confirming it's a gift (not a loan).

Tip: Be ready to document each major deposit or transfer. The more detail you provide, the better. This can include bank statements, legal documents, and any paperwork that explains where the money came from.

3. Proving Legitimacy and Clean Sources

To meet U.S. immigration requirements, you must demonstrate that your funds come from legitimate sources. This typically means avoiding "cash-heavy" sources that might raise suspicions, like large cash deposits without clear origin. Most investors use assets from business income, investments, property sales, or other traceable sources.

Anecdote: Avoiding Cash Red Flags

One investor from Argentina almost ran into trouble when a portion of her funds came from cash deposits with limited documentation. Fortunately, she was able to demonstrate that the deposits were from her family's restaurant, but it was a close call. This experience serves as a reminder that cash-based sources can complicate the process, so always aim for transparent, trackable sources of funds.

Tip: Stick to traceable financial sources wherever possible. If any funds come from less conventional sources, consult with an immigration attorney to ensure you're documenting them adequately.

Calculating Investment Needs: Practical Guide to Estimate Expenses, Investment Thresholds, and Working Capital

Beyond gathering your initial capital, you need to accurately calculate the total investment required to get your business up and running. This step involves estimating the start-up costs, initial operating expenses, and working capital necessary to sustain the business through its early stages.

1. Estimating Start-Up Expenses

Every business has unique start-up costs, so the key here is to understand what's necessary for your specific industry. For a retail store, these costs might include inventory, leasing a storefront, and equipment. For a tech start-up, they might involve software development, marketing, and office space. Start-up costs give U.S. immigration officials insight into your commitment level, as the E-2 visa is designed for investors who make substantial and necessary investments.

Example: Estimating Start-Up Costs for a Small Café

Consider an entrepreneur planning to open a café in Chicago. Start-up expenses might include renovating the space, purchasing furniture, kitchen equipment, and initial supplies, totaling around $150,000. By calculating these expenses, the investor can determine what's necessary to operate the café and demonstrate a "substantial" investment.

Tip: Make a detailed list of start-up costs, including one-time expenses and ongoing operating needs. Use this as the foundation of your financial plan to ensure your investment aligns with business requirements.

2. Determining Investment Thresholds

As we discussed in Chapter 1, the E-2 visa requires a "substantial" investment, but that amount varies based on the type and scale of the business. For smaller, less capital-intensive businesses, the threshold might be lower than for larger ventures. The goal is to show that your investment covers essential needs and that you're financially committed to the business's success.

Anecdote: How an Investor Determined "Substantial" for a Franchise

An E-2 investor from Japan decided to open a franchise location for a fast-food chain. His initial costs included the franchise fee, leasing, renovations, and staffing, totaling around $200,000. Since franchises often require higher upfront costs, he ensured that his investment was substantial enough to support both start-up and operational needs.

Tip: Look up typical start-up costs for your industry to get a sense of what "substantial" might mean. You don't need to over-invest, but it should reflect a serious commitment.

3. Preparing for Working Capital Needs

Beyond start-up expenses, you'll need working capital to cover ongoing costs like salaries, utilities, rent, and inventory replenishment. This is especially important in the early stages, as it can take time for the business to start generating consistent revenue. Working capital provides a cushion that allows the business to operate smoothly and ensures you meet visa requirements.

Example: Calculating Working Capital for a Boutique Store

A boutique store owner estimates monthly expenses, including rent, utilities, payroll, and inventory restocking, to be about $8,000. With this estimate, she sets aside six months' worth of working capital—$48,000—to cover initial operating needs until the store becomes self-sustaining. This careful planning reassures immigration officials that the business is viable and well-prepared.

Tip: Budget for at least six months of working capital as part of your initial investment. This ensures your business can operate smoothly and demonstrates financial planning to U.S. authorities.

Risk Assessment and Business Viability: Factors to Consider for Business Success and Securing Visa Renewals

Starting a business is inherently risky, and with the E-2 visa, your ability to stay in the U.S. depends on that business's success. That's why it's essential to assess potential risks and ensure your business plan is viable over the long term.

1. Evaluating Industry Risks

Consider the industry you're entering. Some industries, like technology and e-commerce, have significant growth potential but also face high competition. Others, like hospitality or retail, may have different risks based on location, customer demand, and seasonality. Understanding these risks can help you make informed decisions and plan accordingly.

Anecdote: Choosing a Low-Risk Business for E-2 Stability

An investor from France chose to start a laundry service in a residential area of New York. Her reasoning was simple: people always need clean clothes, so the business had steady demand. Although it wasn't the most glamorous option, it provided stable income and minimized risk, allowing her to focus on building a reliable, long-term business.

Tip: Research industry trends, customer demand, and potential challenges for your business. Choose a sector that aligns with both your interests and long-term stability goals.

2. Understanding Business Requirements for E-2 Renewal

The E-2 visa is typically issued for two to five years and can be renewed indefinitely as long as the business remains active and profitable. This means you'll need to maintain regular documentation showing the business's performance, profitability, and compliance with visa requirements. Regularly assessing your business's financial health can help ensure your E-2 visa stays in good standing.

Tip: Keep track of revenue, expenses, and job creation data. This documentation will help demonstrate your business's success and provide a foundation for E-2 renewal applications.

3. Preparing for Economic Downturns

Every business faces tough times, whether due to market shifts, economic downturns, or unexpected events. To minimize the impact of these challenges, build a financial buffer and consider flexible business strategies. This preparation can keep your business steady and your E-2 visa secure.

Example: Adapting a Restaurant to Delivery During a Crisis

During the COVID-19 pandemic, an E-2 investor who owned a restaurant in Los Angeles shifted to a delivery-only model to maintain revenue. By adapting to the circumstances, he kept the business afloat and continued meeting E-2 requirements. This agility proved essential to his visa's security during challenging times.

Tip: Build flexibility into your business plan. Consider alternative revenue streams or backup strategies that can help maintain profitability during tough times.

Long-Term Considerations: Lifestyle, Potential for Renewal, and Possibilities for Permanent Residency

The E-2 visa offers the opportunity to live and work in the U.S., but it's essential to consider long-term factors that impact your lifestyle and residency plans.

1. Planning for Lifestyle Changes

Relocating to a new country, especially with family, involves significant lifestyle changes. From adapting to a new culture to finding schools for children, the transition can be exciting but challenging. Setting realistic expectations and preparing for these changes can ease the process.

Anecdote: Lifestyle Adjustments for an E-2 Family

A family from Italy moved to Austin, Texas, for an E-2 investment in a local bakery. Adjusting to a new culture and lifestyle took time, but they gradually adapted by getting involved in local community events and enrolling their children in nearby schools. Embracing the local lifestyle enriched their experience and strengthened their connection to their new home.

Tip: Explore the local area and build connections with other families or entrepreneurs. This can make the transition easier and help you feel at home in your new environment.

2. Renewal and Long-Term Residency Plans

The E-2 visa can be renewed indefinitely as long as the business is active and profitable. However, because it doesn't lead to a green card or citizenship, it's worth considering other residency options if you plan to stay long-term. Many E-2 holders eventually explore pathways like the EB-5 investor visa, employment-based green cards, or family sponsorship if they're eligible.

Tip: Consult with an immigration attorney about options for permanent residency. Understanding your choices early on can help you plan a long-term strategy.

3. Exit Strategy and Financial Security

It's wise to have an exit strategy, whether that means selling the business, transitioning to a different visa, or moving back to your home country. Having a plan in place ensures you're financially secure regardless of where your journey takes you.

Tip: Regularly assess your business's performance and consider potential exit strategies. This helps you stay prepared and flexible, whether you continue renewing your E-2 or transition to other opportunities.

Bringing It All Together

Setting realistic personal and financial expectations is key to making the E-2 visa journey a success. By preparing your finances, understanding the investment requirements, evaluating risks, and planning for the future, you're building a solid foundation for both your business and your life in the U.S.

Remember, the E-2 visa isn't just about capital—it's about commitment, resilience, and adaptability. With a well-prepared plan and clear expectations, you'll be ready to take on the opportunities and challenges that come with being an E-2 investor in the United States.

Part 2: Structuring Your E-2 Investment

CHAPTER 3: CHOOSING THE RIGHT BUSINESS MODEL FOR E-2 INVESTMENT

Choosing the right business model is one of the most important decisions you'll make as an E-2 investor. Your choice isn't just about finding a profitable venture; it's about finding a model that aligns with your skills, interests, and visa requirements. Some investors choose to start a business from scratch, while others prefer buying an existing business or investing in a franchise. Each option comes with its own pros and cons, and finding the right fit for your E-2 journey can make all the difference.

This chapter will walk you through the different business models available to E-2 investors. We'll look at starting a new business versus acquiring an existing one, the unique benefits of franchises, and the importance of choosing an active business type. We'll also explore popular industries for E-2 investors, giving you insight into the types of businesses that tend to work well for this visa. Let's dive in!

Starting a New Business vs. Acquisition: Pros, Cons, and E-2 Compliance for Each Option

One of the first questions E-2 investors face is whether to start a business from scratch or acquire an existing one. Each option has its own set of advantages and challenges, and the right choice depends on your goals, experience, and tolerance for risk.

1. Starting a New Business

Starting a business from scratch allows you to build something uniquely yours, creating a brand, products, and services that reflect your vision. This path is ideal for entrepreneurs who have a clear idea for a business and are excited to create something new. Starting a business from scratch also allows you to structure the business specifically to meet E-2 requirements, ensuring active involvement from the start.

Pros:

- **Creative Freedom:** You get to design every aspect of the business, from branding to product offerings.
- **Customization for E-2 Compliance:** Since you're building from the ground up, it's easier to ensure the business aligns with E-2 requirements for active management.
- **Potential for Higher Returns:** With a successful business model, you have the potential for high returns as the business grows.

Cons:

- **Higher Risk:** Starting from scratch comes with a higher risk of failure, as new businesses face challenges like market entry and brand recognition.
- **Longer Timeline:** It takes time to establish a new business, build a customer base, and generate consistent revenue.
- **More Work Upfront:** You'll need to handle every detail, from market research and business planning to hiring and operations.

Anecdote: The Journey of Starting Fresh with an E-2

One E-2 investor I know from Italy started a boutique coffee shop in New York. She loved the idea of creating a space that felt like home, and she spent months planning the design, menu, and sourcing Italian coffee beans. Although she faced plenty of challenges in the beginning—finding a good location, marketing to local customers—she built a loyal following over time. This story highlights both the excitement and hard work that come with starting a new business from scratch.

Tip: If you have a unique business idea and enjoy building from the ground up, starting a new business can be rewarding. Just be prepared for a learning curve and keep in mind that it might take time to become profitable.

2. Acquiring an Existing Business

Buying an existing business can be a faster path to E-2 investment, as it allows you to step into an established operation with customers, revenue, and potentially a solid reputation. For investors looking to reduce risk, an acquisition can be a practical choice, as you're buying into a business model that already works.

Pros:

- **Immediate Revenue:** Existing businesses usually have an established customer base, making it easier to generate revenue from day one.
- **Reduced Risk:** Acquiring a business with a proven track record can reduce the uncertainty associated with start-ups.
- **Easier Financing Options:** Banks are sometimes more willing to lend to buyers of established businesses, as they're seen as lower risk.

Cons:

- **Higher Upfront Cost:** Acquiring an established business often requires a larger upfront investment compared to starting from scratch.
- **Potential for Hidden Issues:** Inherited challenges, such as unprofitable contracts or difficult employees, can complicate the transition.
- **Less Creative Control:** You're inheriting a business structure, brand, and customer base, which may limit your ability to make changes.

Case Study: The Benefits of Buying a Proven Business

An E-2 investor from Japan bought an existing flower shop in California. By acquiring a business with an established reputation and customer base, he was able to generate income immediately and avoid the high start-up costs associated with a new business. This allowed him to focus on gradual improvements, like expanding the delivery area and adding new products. By starting with an established foundation, he minimized risk and found a quicker path to profitability.

Tip: If you're looking for a more stable entry into the U.S. market, consider acquiring a business. Look for an operation with a proven track record, and conduct thorough due diligence to uncover any potential issues.

Exploring Franchises: Benefits and Risks, Popular E-2-Friendly Franchises, and How Franchises Can Simplify the E-2 Process

Franchises offer a middle ground between starting a new business and acquiring an existing one. When you buy a franchise, you're purchasing the rights to operate under a brand's established name, using their business model, marketing, and training. For E-2 investors, franchises can be an appealing option because they provide a clear structure, brand recognition, and support that make it easier to meet E-2 requirements.

1. Benefits of Franchises for E-2 Investors

Franchises offer several advantages, especially for investors new to the U.S. business environment.

- **Proven Business Model:** Franchises come with a tested business model, reducing the risk associated with start-ups.
- **Support and Training:** Franchisors provide training, marketing support, and operational guidance, helping you get started quickly.
- **Brand Recognition:** Established franchises come with built-in brand awareness, making it easier to attract customers.

Anecdote: How a Franchise Provided a Head Start

A Canadian E-2 investor opened a popular fitness franchise in Texas. With no prior experience in the fitness industry, he benefited from the franchisor's training program, which included everything from operations to marketing. This support allowed him to focus on managing the business without feeling overwhelmed by industry knowledge gaps.

Tip: Franchises are a great option if you're looking for structure and support. Just ensure the franchise aligns with your interests and skills.

2. Risks of Franchises

While franchises offer a solid foundation, they also come with certain limitations.

- **Franchise Fees:** Buying into a franchise requires paying initial fees, and some franchises have ongoing royalties, which reduce profit margins.
- **Limited Control:** Franchise agreements often come with strict guidelines, limiting your ability to make changes to the business model, pricing, or branding.

- **Dependence on Brand Reputation:** You're tied to the franchisor's reputation. If the brand's reputation suffers, it could affect your business.

Example: Balancing Benefits and Restrictions

An E-2 investor from Mexico opened a fast-casual restaurant franchise. While he appreciated the brand recognition and steady flow of customers, he found the franchisor's restrictions on suppliers and menu changes challenging. This example highlights the importance of understanding the limitations before committing to a franchise.

Tip: Read the franchise agreement carefully to understand all restrictions. Make sure you're comfortable with the brand's requirements and limitations before making a commitment.

3. Popular E-2-Friendly Franchises

Certain franchises are especially popular among E-2 investors due to their manageable entry costs and supportive franchise networks. These include brands like Subway, Anytime Fitness, and Kumon Learning Centers. Look for franchises that align with your interests and budget, as a well-suited franchise can simplify the E-2 application process by offering proven business systems and support.

Tip: Research franchise options with a track record of supporting E-2 investors. Many franchises are familiar with the E-2 requirements and can help make the application process smoother.

Alternative Business Models: Passive vs. Active Business Types, and Ensuring Active Involvement to Satisfy E-2 Requirements

The E-2 visa requires active involvement, so it's crucial to choose a business model that allows you to play an ongoing, hands-on role. While some businesses, like rental properties, may seem appealing, they often don't meet E-2 requirements unless you're actively managing the operations.

1. Passive vs. Active Businesses

Passive businesses, like stocks, rental properties, or investment funds, don't qualify for the E-2 because they lack active management. The E-2 visa is designed for investors who contribute to a business's day-to-day operations, making active involvement essential. However, certain types of real estate, like property management, can qualify if you're actively involved in managing properties, coordinating maintenance, and handling tenant relationships.

Anecdote: Transitioning from Passive to Active Management

An investor from Australia initially planned to buy a rental property to qualify for an E-2 visa. However, he quickly realized this wouldn't meet the active involvement requirement. Instead, he shifted to property management, actively overseeing maintenance, tenant relations, and marketing. This adjustment allowed him to qualify by demonstrating his active role in the business.

Tip: Be wary of passive investments. Choose a model that allows for hands-on involvement, whether that's managing employees, coordinating with clients, or making strategic decisions.

2. Examples of Active Business Types

To ensure your E-2 application meets requirements, consider active businesses like consulting, hospitality, or retail. These industries require continuous management, allowing you to demonstrate that you're directly involved in operations.

Example: Consulting Firm as an Active Business

A consulting firm provides professional services that require ongoing client interactions, project management, and strategy development. An E-2 investor who starts a consulting business can easily demonstrate active involvement, making it an ideal option for meeting visa requirements.

Tip: Choose a business type that requires regular decision-making and management. Active businesses not only qualify for the E-2 visa but also offer more opportunities for growth and long-term success.

Popular Industries for E-2 Investors: Profiles of Industries Well-Suited for E-2, Including Real Estate, Hospitality, Consulting, and Retail

Certain industries are particularly well-suited for E-2 investors due to their active nature, manageable entry costs, and market demand. Let's look at some popular options.

1. Real Estate Management

Real estate management, as opposed to passive real estate investments, can qualify for E-2 if you're actively managing properties. This includes tenant relations, property maintenance, and leasing. Real estate management businesses can be profitable and offer stability, particularly in growing markets.

2. Hospitality and Food Services

Restaurants, cafés, and hospitality businesses are popular among E-2 investors because they require hands-on involvement. These businesses offer a high level of customer interaction and allow you to demonstrate active management, from staffing to daily operations.

3. Consulting and Professional Services

If you have expertise in a specific field, consulting can be an ideal choice. Consulting firms allow you to work directly with clients, handle project management, and make strategic decisions. This model is highly flexible, allowing you to leverage your skills while meeting E-2 requirements.

4. Retail and E-Commerce

Retail businesses, including e-commerce, can be suitable for E-2 investors looking to manage operations, inventory, and customer service. Whether you're selling products online or through a physical store, retail allows for flexibility and active involvement.

Tip: Consider industries that align with your experience and interests. A well-suited industry not only helps with E-2 compliance but also enhances your chances of long-term success.

Bringing It All Together

Choosing the right business model for your E-2 investment is a critical decision that impacts your visa application, business success, and personal satisfaction. Whether you're interested in starting from scratch, buying an existing business, or exploring franchise options, the right choice will align with your skills, budget, and goals.

By understanding the pros and cons of each option, exploring franchise possibilities, and choosing an active business model, you'll set yourself up for a successful E-2 journey. Remember, the best business model is one that not only fulfills E-2 requirements but also allows you to create a rewarding and sustainable venture in the United States.

CHAPTER 4: FORMING PARTNERSHIPS, JOINT VENTURES, AND ALTERNATIVE STRUCTURES

Forming partnerships and exploring alternative structures like joint ventures or investment groups can be excellent ways to meet E-2 requirements while sharing risk, maximizing resources, and enhancing your potential for success. For many E-2 investors, co-investing with others or forming a joint venture can provide the financial stability and support needed to enter the U.S. market more confidently. However, working within these structures requires careful planning to ensure you retain the necessary level of control and active management required by the E-2 visa.

In this chapter, we'll explore various ways to structure your E-2 investment using partnerships, joint ventures, and investment groups. We'll also discuss the advantages of setting up your business as an LLC or corporation and the unique considerations each structure brings. Whether you're co-investing with a friend, joining an investment group, or entering into a joint venture, this chapter will guide you through strategies for building a successful E-2 investment while maintaining compliance with visa requirements.

Using Partnerships to Meet E-2 Requirements: Structuring Majority Control While Co-Investing

Many E-2 investors find that entering the U.S. market is easier when they share the investment load with a partner. Partnerships allow you to pool resources, skills, and expertise while meeting E-2 requirements, as long as you maintain majority control and active involvement in the business. Structuring a partnership can be a great way to balance financial risk, provided you understand the importance of retaining control over the business.

1. Why Partnerships Work for E-2 Investors

When you partner with another investor, you can share the financial burden, expand your resources, and leverage each other's expertise. However, the E-2 visa requires that you, as the visa holder, maintain at least 50% control over the business and take an active role in its management. This means structuring your partnership in a way that provides you with decision-making authority.

Case Study: Balancing Control in a Café Partnership

I once worked with two friends from Canada who wanted to open a café in Los Angeles. To reduce their financial risk, they decided to split the investment, but since only one was applying for the E-2 visa, they structured the partnership so that the E-2 applicant retained 60% ownership. This allowed the E-2 applicant to meet visa requirements while both partners contributed capital, shared operational roles, and brought their unique skills to the business.

Tip: Make sure your partnership agreement clearly outlines each person's role, investment, and decision-making power. Having an agreement in writing can help prevent conflicts down the road and demonstrates to immigration authorities that you retain active control.

2. Structuring Partnerships for Majority Control

In E-2 partnerships, retaining majority control doesn't just mean having the most shares; it also involves having the authority to make key business decisions. Structuring your partnership with a "majority member" designation for the E-2 applicant can establish that you're the primary decision-maker in the business, meeting visa requirements.

Example: Structuring for Control in a Retail Business

An E-2 investor from France partnered with a U.S. citizen to open a clothing boutique. They set up a 51/49 ownership structure, with the E-2 investor holding the majority. To reinforce the E-2 applicant's control, they included terms in their partnership agreement granting the E-2 investor decision-making authority over major business operations, such as hiring, purchasing, and strategic planning. This not only protected the investor's visa status but also ensured they had the influence necessary to guide the business's success.

Tip: Consult an attorney when drafting partnership agreements. U.S. immigration officials will scrutinize your role and control within the business, so it's important to have a clear and legally sound structure.

Joint Ventures for Diversified Investments: Balancing Risk and Maintaining an Active Role

Joint ventures (JVs) are another option for E-2 investors interested in diversifying their investment and spreading out risk. A JV allows you to partner with other investors or businesses, combining resources to enter new markets or tackle larger projects. For E-2 purposes, it's essential that you remain actively involved in the JV's operations to satisfy visa requirements.

1. How Joint Ventures Can Benefit E-2 Investors

Joint ventures offer a way to participate in large-scale projects without shouldering all the risk yourself. They can be particularly beneficial if you're entering an industry that requires significant upfront investment or specialized expertise. With a JV, you're not just splitting costs; you're also gaining access to your partner's network, experience, and resources. This can help you expand faster and with greater stability.

Example: A Real Estate Joint Venture

A pair of E-2 investors from South Korea formed a JV to develop a commercial property in Florida. They partnered with a U.S.-based developer who provided local knowledge and operational support. Each E-2 investor took an active role in overseeing construction, coordinating with contractors, and managing finances, ensuring they met visa requirements while leveraging the developer's expertise. This setup allowed them to participate in a high-value project with reduced individual financial exposure.

Tip: In a joint venture, clearly define each party's role and responsibilities to avoid conflicts and ensure everyone is contributing to the business's success. Make sure your role aligns with the E-2 requirement for active management.

2. Maintaining an Active Role in a Joint Venture

One of the most important aspects of a JV for E-2 investors is ensuring that your role is more than financial. As an E-2 visa holder, you need to demonstrate that you're actively involved in day-to-day operations, such as project management, strategic planning, or team coordination. If your role becomes passive, you risk losing visa compliance.

Case Study: Active Involvement in a Restaurant JV

A German E-2 investor joined a joint venture to open a farm-to-table restaurant in San Diego. Although he didn't have experience in the restaurant industry, he took on the responsibility of overseeing the supply chain, building relationships with local farmers, and managing inventory. His active involvement in sourcing and supplier management satisfied E-2 requirements and made him an integral part of the business's success.

Tip: Identify specific areas within the joint venture where your skills and expertise can add value. This ensures your role remains active and impactful, demonstrating your commitment to the business.

Working with Investment Groups or Funds: How to Invest Within a Group While Meeting E-2 Active Management Requirements

Investment groups or funds are popular ways to pool resources for larger ventures, such as real estate developments or tech startups. However, meeting E-2 requirements within a group can be tricky, as the visa necessitates that you play an active role in management, not just financial investment.

1. Structuring Your Role in an Investment Group

To qualify for an E-2 visa while participating in an investment group, you'll need to hold a managerial role or be directly involved in operational decisions. Unlike traditional investors in a fund, E-2 applicants cannot take a hands-off approach. Instead, you might consider structuring your role as a project manager, operational supervisor, or another active position that aligns with E-2 criteria.

Example: Active Involvement in a Real Estate Investment Group

An E-2 investor from Mexico joined a real estate investment group focused on multi-family housing. Rather than simply contributing capital, he took on the role of property manager, overseeing maintenance, leasing, and tenant relations. By establishing a formal position within the group, he was able to maintain compliance with E-2 requirements while benefiting from the resources and expertise of the group.

Tip: Choose an investment group where you can take on an active operational role. If your position involves decision-making or project management, you'll be more likely to meet E-2 guidelines.

2. Choosing Investment Groups That Fit E-2 Requirements

Some investment groups cater specifically to E-2 visa investors, offering roles that ensure active management. These groups are familiar with the visa's requirements and structure positions accordingly, which can simplify the process. Look for groups that offer specific job functions, such as overseeing operations, managing client relations, or handling finance.

Anecdote: Finding the Right Investment Group

One E-2 investor I know from the UK found an investment group specializing in boutique hotels. The group needed someone to manage guest services and marketing, so the investor took on these responsibilities. Not only did this role allow him to satisfy E-2 requirements, but it also allowed him to use his hospitality background, making the investment both compliant and fulfilling.

Tip: Research investment groups that are experienced with E-2 investors. They may be better equipped to offer roles that align with visa requirements.

Leveraging LLCs and Corporations: Differences Between Structures, Control, and Tax Implications

Choosing the right business structure is essential for E-2 investors. While both LLCs and corporations offer limited liability and the ability to attract co-investors, they come with different tax implications, control options, and operational flexibility. Understanding these differences can help you make an informed choice that aligns with your investment goals and visa requirements.

1. LLCs: Flexibility and Pass-Through Taxation

Limited Liability Companies (LLCs) are popular among E-2 investors due to their flexibility and pass-through taxation, meaning profits and losses are reported on the owner's personal tax return. LLCs also offer flexibility in management structure, allowing you to customize roles and responsibilities within the business.

Example: Using an LLC for a Consulting Firm

An E-2 investor from Italy started a consulting firm as an LLC in New York. The pass-through taxation allowed him to avoid double taxation, and the LLC structure gave him flexibility in managing the firm. By setting up the LLC as a "member-managed" entity, he demonstrated his active involvement, meeting E-2 requirements.

Tip: LLCs can be a good choice if you want tax simplicity and flexibility in business management. However, consult a tax advisor to understand how LLC taxes will apply to your specific situation as a non-U.S. citizen.

2. Corporations: Ideal for Larger Ventures

Corporations are often chosen for larger ventures with multiple investors. Unlike LLCs, corporations are separate taxable entities, which means profits are taxed at the corporate level. However, corporations may be beneficial if you're seeking outside investment or plan to scale the business significantly.

Case Study: Corporation Structure for a Tech Startup

A tech entrepreneur from Canada formed a corporation to

launch a software development company. He anticipated needing multiple rounds of investment and preferred the corporate structure for its ability to issue stock. As the majority shareholder and CEO, he met E-2 requirements by actively overseeing product development and managing the business.

Tip: If you plan to grow your business significantly or seek external investment, a corporation may provide more options. Just be prepared for corporate tax responsibilities.

3. Tax Considerations and Control

Understanding the tax implications of your chosen structure is essential, as taxes can differ significantly between LLCs and corporations. Consult a tax advisor to evaluate which structure best suits your financial goals, especially if you're planning to reinvest profits or distribute dividends.

Anecdote: Navigating Taxes with an LLC

One investor I know from Australia initially set up a corporation, but later switched to an LLC due to high corporate tax rates. This move simplified his tax obligations and aligned better with his goal of reinvesting profits into the business, ultimately helping him meet both E-2 requirements and financial goals.

Tip: Weigh tax implications carefully. The right structure can help you maximize profits while staying compliant with U.S. tax laws and E-2 requirements.

Bringing It All Together

Forming partnerships, joint ventures, or using alternative structures like LLCs and corporations offers diverse options for structuring your E-2 investment. Each approach has unique advantages, and the right choice depends on your goals, risk tolerance, and the type of involvement you want in your business.

By understanding the requirements for E-2 compliance, structuring partnerships thoughtfully, and choosing the appropriate business entity, you'll be well-positioned to build a successful and compliant business. Whether you're partnering with others, joining a joint venture, or setting up a corporate entity, these strategies will help you create a foundation that supports your investment and E-2 goals.

CHAPTER 5: CRAFTING A WINNING BUSINESS PLAN

When applying for an E-2 visa, your business plan is more than just a roadmap for your business—it's a critical component of your application. Think of it as your chance to show U.S. Citizenship and Immigration Services (USCIS) that your business idea is viable, well-thought-out, and has the potential to contribute to the local economy. A strong business plan can mean the difference between approval and denial, so taking the time to craft a detailed, compelling plan is essential.

In this chapter, we'll cover why a business plan is so important for E-2 applications, walk through the essential sections, share tips on how to present it effectively, and dive into how to set realistic financial projections and job creation goals. With some guidance and a little strategy, you'll be ready to put together a business plan that makes a strong case for your E-2 application.

Purpose of a Business Plan in E-2 Applications: Importance for the Visa Application Process

The business plan you submit for an E-2 application isn't just about convincing yourself or potential investors that your business can succeed; it's about showing immigration officials that your business is a serious, sustainable endeavor. USCIS wants to know that your business has real potential to contribute to the U.S. economy through job creation, economic impact, and growth potential.

1. Why USCIS Cares About Your Business Plan

USCIS reviews your business plan to assess the viability and sustainability of your business. They're looking to see that your investment is sufficient, that you'll be actively involved in managing the business, and that the business can generate revenue and create jobs. A solid business plan proves that you're prepared, serious about your investment, and capable of running a successful operation in the U.S.

Anecdote: The Case of the Café with a Plan

I once worked with an E-2 applicant from Brazil who wanted to open a small café in Seattle. Her business plan wasn't just about coffee; it outlined a unique concept focused on locally sourced ingredients and sustainable practices. USCIS loved her detailed plan, particularly her focus on job creation and environmental impact. Her business plan not only secured her visa but also laid out a clear roadmap for her café's success. This story underscores the value of a well-crafted plan that goes beyond the basics.

Tip: Think of your business plan as your first impression with USCIS. Show them that you've done your homework and have a realistic, well-thought-out strategy for success.

2. Establishing Credibility and Commitment

A strong business plan also demonstrates your commitment to the business. USCIS wants to see that you're fully invested and serious about building something sustainable, not just looking for a temporary foothold in the U.S. Your business plan should reflect this commitment, highlighting the time, money, and resources you're ready to invest in making the business work.

Tip: Emphasize your dedication to building and growing the business. Details on long-term plans, like expanding product lines or opening additional locations, show USCIS that you're in it for the long haul.

Key Sections of the E-2 Business Plan: Market Analysis, Competition, Job Creation, Financial Projections

An effective E-2 business plan has several core sections that provide a complete picture of your business. Let's walk through each one, looking at what USCIS wants to see and how you can make each section stand out.

1. Executive Summary

The executive summary is your introduction. It should be short, engaging, and to the point, covering the essentials: what your business does, where it's located, and why it's viable. This section should grab the reader's attention and give a snapshot of what's to come.

Tip: Write your executive summary last. By the time you've finished your plan, you'll have a clearer idea of the highlights to include in your summary.

2. Market Analysis

Market analysis is where you show that you understand the industry, your target market, and the demand for your product or service. USCIS wants to see that you've done your research and know what it will take to succeed in your chosen market.

Example: Market Analysis for a Fitness Studio

Imagine you're opening a fitness studio in Austin. Your market analysis could include details about the city's health-conscious population, trends in fitness spending, and growth in boutique fitness. By showing data on the increasing demand for specialized fitness studios, you demonstrate that your business has a solid market foundation.

Tip: Use data to support your points. Show USCIS you're basing your plan on real research, not just assumptions.

3. Competitive Analysis

USCIS will want to know who your competitors are and what sets your business apart. A competitive analysis shows that you're aware of existing players in your field and have a strategy for standing out. This section can include direct competitors, like similar local businesses, and indirect competitors, like online alternatives.

Anecdote: Standing Out in a Competitive Market

An E-2 investor from Germany planned to open a specialty bakery in a busy neighborhood with several bakeries already in operation. In her business plan, she included a competitive analysis that highlighted her bakery's unique selling point: vegan and gluten-free options not offered by competitors. This distinction helped USCIS see how her bakery could attract a specific customer base despite the competition.

Tip: Emphasize what makes you unique. Show USCIS that you understand the market landscape and have a clear way to differentiate your business.

4. Job Creation Goals

Job creation is a critical part of the E-2 application, as USCIS wants to see that your business will positively impact the local economy. Detail how many jobs you plan to create, what roles these employees will fill, and when you'll start hiring.

Example: Job Creation in a Restaurant

A restaurant business plan could outline job creation in phases, starting with kitchen and wait staff, followed by a marketing manager and part-time support staff as the business grows. This phased approach shows USCIS that you have a realistic plan to support job creation over time.

Tip: Be specific. Name the types of positions, projected salaries, and timelines to show USCIS that you have a clear hiring strategy.

5. Financial Projections

Financial projections are essential for showing that your business can be profitable. They include revenue forecasts, projected expenses, and anticipated profits over the next three to five years. USCIS wants to know that your business can sustain itself and generate enough revenue to support your investment.

Case Study: Financial Projections for a Tech Start-Up

An E-2 applicant from India created financial projections for his tech start-up that included revenue from app subscriptions, advertising, and corporate partnerships. His projections demonstrated not only initial profitability but also a clear path for growth, which helped him make a convincing case to USCIS.

Tip: Keep your projections realistic. Inflated numbers can raise red flags. It's better to present conservative, achievable estimates that align with industry standards.

Presentation Tips: Formatting, Language, and Elements That USCIS Emphasizes

A business plan that's well-organized and easy to read will make a stronger impression. Remember, USCIS reviewers are reading through a lot of material, so clarity and professionalism go a long way.

1. Formatting for Readability

Use headings, bullet points, and short paragraphs to make your business plan easy to navigate. A cluttered or confusing layout can be a barrier, so focus on clean, simple formatting that guides the reader through each section.

Tip: Include a table of contents with page numbers. This makes it easier for USCIS officials to find specific sections and shows that your plan is professionally organized.

2. Using Clear, Professional Language

Your business plan should be concise and professional, free from jargon or overly complex language. Avoid fluff and stick to the facts, as USCIS is more interested in clear, actionable information than persuasive language.

Example: Plain Language in Market Analysis

Instead of saying, "The fitness industry is on fire, with trends going through the roof," opt for something like, "According to industry reports, the fitness industry is expected to grow by X % over the next five years, demonstrating sustained demand for health-focused services."

Tip: Use straightforward language that communicates your message clearly. If possible, have a native English speaker review your plan for clarity and flow.

3. Highlighting Elements USCIS Prioritizes

USCIS pays particular attention to financial viability, job creation, and active management, so make sure these sections are strong. For example, be thorough with financial projections and provide as much detail as possible in the job creation section.

Anecdote: Highlighting Key Elements for USCIS

An E-2 investor from South Korea put extra emphasis on the job creation section of his business plan, as he planned to open a new restaurant with high staffing needs. He included timelines, estimated wages, and job descriptions, which helped USCIS see the immediate economic impact his business would have on the community.

Tip: If you're not sure what USCIS values most, ask yourself, "Does this section show that my business will contribute positively to the local economy?" Focusing on impact and sustainability can help you emphasize key points.

Financial Projections and Job Creation Goals: Setting Realistic Targets That Meet Both Business and E-2 Needs

Financial projections and job creation are core to the E-2 application. These

numbers demonstrate the business's viability and its potential to support the local economy. Setting achievable, well-supported targets can strengthen your business plan and boost your chances of approval.

1. Setting Realistic Financial Projections

Your financial projections should cover revenue, expenses, and profits over three to five years. Be realistic—exaggerated numbers can make your business look less credible. Use data from your market analysis to support revenue estimates, and include a detailed breakdown of expenses.

Case Study: Conservative Projections for a Retail Store

A British E-2 applicant opening a retail store in Miami created projections based on average revenue per square foot for stores in similar locations. By keeping her numbers conservative and tying them to market data, she presented a credible case to USCIS. Her conservative approach also made it easier to meet her projections, building confidence with USCIS in her business's potential.

Tip: Ground your projections in industry data whenever possible. Show USCIS that you're not just guessing, but basing your numbers on real, research-backed information.

2. Job Creation Goals Aligned with E-2 Requirements

USCIS is interested in businesses that will create jobs for American workers. When setting job creation goals, aim to outline roles that are essential to your business's growth. Show when you plan to hire and how each role will contribute to the business.

Example: Job Creation Plan for an IT Consulting Firm

An E-2 applicant starting an IT consulting firm planned to hire two employees in the first year and two more in the second year. He included job descriptions and projected salaries, explaining how each role would help expand client services. This concrete job plan gave USCIS confidence in his commitment to local job creation.

Tip: Provide specific timelines for hiring. Show that you're thinking about long-term growth and the gradual expansion of your team as your business grows.

Bringing It All Together

Creating a compelling business plan for your E-2 application is all about combining thorough research with realistic goals. Your business plan should give USCIS a clear, confident picture of your business's potential, from market opportunities and competitive advantages to job creation and financial projections.

Remember, the business plan isn't just a formality—it's your chance to make a case for why your business belongs in the U.S. By following the tips in this chapter and putting care into every section, you'll be well on your way to crafting a business plan that not only secures your visa but also sets your business up for success.

Part 3: The E-2 Visa Application Process

CHAPTER 6: COMPILING REQUIRED DOCUMENTATION

Applying for an E-2 visa is exciting, but it's also paperwork-heavy. Compiling the required documentation can seem overwhelming, but with the right preparation, you can tackle this step-by-step and avoid unnecessary stress. This chapter is all about helping you get organized, so you know exactly what documents you need, why they matter, and how to present them in a way that supports your application.

Let's walk through the essential documents checklist, explore how to prove the legitimacy of your investment funds, look at supporting business documents, and learn how to demonstrate your intent to actively manage the business. Think of this as your documentation roadmap for a successful E-2 application.

Essential Documents Checklist: Forms, Financial Evidence, and Business Documentation

A strong E-2 application requires a comprehensive set of documents that provide USCIS or the consulate with a full picture of your business, investment, and intentions. While it may feel like a lot, each document serves a purpose and helps build a solid case for your application.

1. Forms and Identification

Start with the basic forms and identification documents. These are straightforward but essential, as they establish your identity and the initial foundation of your application.

- **DS-160 Form**: This is the primary application form for nonimmigrant visas. You'll fill this out online and pay the associated fees, which can vary depending on your country.
- **Passport**: Make sure your passport is valid for at least six months beyond your intended stay. If your family is applying with you, they'll each need a valid passport as well.
- **Passport-Style Photos**: These will be uploaded as part of your application. Check the photo guidelines carefully to ensure they meet USCIS standards.

Tip: Double-check that your name, passport number, and all other details match exactly across all forms. Any discrepancies could delay your application.

2. Financial Evidence

Next, you'll need documents that prove you have the funds necessary to invest in the business, along with proof that these funds were acquired legitimately. USCIS wants to know that your money is legally sourced and that your investment amount is substantial enough to support the business's success.

- **Bank Statements**: These statements should show the funds are available and ready for investment. If the money has been transferred to a U.S. account, include both foreign and U.S. bank statements.
- **Proof of Funds Transfer**: If you've transferred the investment funds into a business account, include wire transfer receipts or bank records showing the transfer.
- **Documentation of Source of Funds**: This could include tax returns, property sale documents, or business

income records, depending on where the funds came from (we'll discuss this more in the next section).

Anecdote: The Case of the Missing Transfer Receipt

One E-2 investor from Germany nearly had his application delayed because he forgot to include the receipt for his wire transfer. USCIS wanted clear proof that his funds had been moved into a U.S. bank account. After a quick scramble to get the receipt, his application went through, but this experience highlights the importance of being thorough with your financial records.

Tip: Include every document that shows the movement of your funds. Missing or incomplete financial documentation can cause delays, so it's better to err on the side of over-preparing.

3. Business Documentation

The business documents are the core of your E-2 application. These demonstrate that your business is legitimate, operational, and aligned with your investment goals. Make sure each document is clear, accurate, and up-to-date.

- **Business Registration**: This could be your LLC or corporation registration document, showing that your business is officially registered and recognized by the state.
- **Employer Identification Number (EIN)**: This IRS-issued number is required for U.S. businesses. It shows that your business is recognized for tax purposes.
- **Lease Agreement**: If you're renting commercial space, include a signed lease to demonstrate your business location. For some businesses, location is critical, and this document reassures USCIS that you're operational.

Example: Using a Lease Agreement to Strengthen an Application

A Canadian E-2 investor opening a boutique clothing store included a signed lease agreement for a storefront in downtown Seattle. This document, combined with her business plan, helped

USCIS see her commitment to establishing a brick-and-mortar presence, which strengthened her application.

Tip: Make sure all business documentation is signed, dated, and fully executed. A draft lease or unsigned document won't carry the same weight as a finalized, legal agreement.

Proof of Legitimate Source of Funds: Best Practices for Providing Clear Financial Documentation

Proving the legitimacy of your funds is crucial for the E-2 visa. USCIS wants to see that your investment comes from legitimate sources—whether it's savings, business income, or an inheritance. A clear and well-organized paper trail will save you from headaches later in the process.

1. Common Sources of Funds and Required Documentation

Your documentation needs to match the origin of your funds, so let's look at some common sources and the paperwork required:

- **Personal Savings**: Bank statements showing consistent deposits over time, backed by tax returns or pay stubs to verify income sources.
- **Business Profits**: If your investment comes from business income, provide tax returns, profit-and-loss statements, and bank statements from your business accounts.
- **Sale of Property**: For property sales, include the sales contract, transfer of title, and bank statements showing the deposited funds.
- **Inheritance**: If you've inherited funds, include the will or inheritance documentation along with bank statements showing the transfer.

Case Study: Documenting Personal Savings for a Clean Paper Trail

An E-2 investor from the UK funded her business with personal savings accumulated over five years. She provided tax returns, bank statements, and pay slips to show a steady accumulation of funds. This detailed documentation reassured USCIS that her investment was legitimate, and her application sailed through without additional questions.

Tip: Make sure your documentation shows a clear, chronological path of your funds. The goal is to make it easy for USCIS to see where your money came from and how it ended up in your U.S. business account.

2. Organizing Your Financial Paperwork

Presenting a well-organized financial document package can make your application easier to review. Use labeled folders or binders with tabs for each source of funds, and provide a cover sheet that explains each section.

Tip: Include a summary page that briefly describes the origin of your funds. This overview can give USCIS a quick understanding of your financial background and make the full documentation easier to review.

3. Addressing Red Flags and Unusual Sources of Funds

If your funds come from an unusual source, like a loan from a family member or a cryptocurrency sale, you'll need additional documentation to clarify the transaction.

Example: Explaining a Family Loan

An investor from Japan funded part of his investment through a loan from his father. To make this clear, he included a signed loan agreement, proof of his father's funds, and bank statements showing the transfer. This transparent approach helped USCIS understand the legitimacy of the loan.

Tip: If you have an unusual source of funds, provide as much detail as possible. Transparency is key when it comes to addressing unique funding sources.

Supporting Business Documents: Licenses, Business Formation Documents, and Lease Agreements

USCIS wants to see that your business is fully operational and legally compliant. This means providing licenses, formation documents, and any agreements related to your business premises.

1. Business Formation Documents

Your business formation documents prove that you've legally established your business in the U.S. These include articles of incorporation, operating agreements, and state registrations.

Example: Ensuring Proper Registration for a Smooth Application

An investor from South Africa formed an LLC for his business consulting firm. He included the LLC's articles of organization and operating agreement in his application, demonstrating to USCIS that his business was properly registered and compliant with state laws.

Tip: Make sure all formation documents are complete and signed. Missing or incomplete documents could raise questions about your business's legitimacy.

2. Required Business Licenses and Permits

Depending on your industry, you may need specific licenses or permits to operate legally. For example, a restaurant requires health permits, while a construction business may need contractor licenses. USCIS wants to see that your business complies with local and state regulations.

Case Study: Licenses for a Catering Business

An E-2 applicant from Australia opening a catering business in Los Angeles included her catering license, food handling certification, and health department permits in her application. This thorough approach reassured USCIS that her business was fully licensed and ready to operate.

Tip: Research the specific licenses required for your business type. Providing these documents can strengthen your application by showing that you're prepared and compliant.

3. Lease Agreements and Premises Documentation

If your business operates from a physical location, a signed lease agreement or property ownership document is essential. For home-based businesses, be prepared to explain how your business meets operational needs without a storefront.

Tip: For physical premises, include photographs of your location along with the lease agreement. Visuals can help USCIS understand the scale and setup of your business.

Showing Intent to Develop and Direct: How to Document and Prove an Active Managerial Role

USCIS requires that E-2 investors actively manage their business, not just invest money and walk away. To meet this requirement, include documents that demonstrate your intent to develop and direct the business.

1. Job Titles and Responsibilities

Your application should include a description of your role within the business, highlighting your duties, job title, and how you'll oversee daily operations. This can include creating budgets, hiring staff, managing client relationships, and setting business strategies.

Example: Documenting a Managerial Role in a Consulting Firm

An investor from Italy starting a consulting firm included a job description that outlined her role in client acquisition, project oversight, and financial planning. She provided examples of specific tasks she'd manage, such as creating client proposals and overseeing service delivery, to show USCIS her hands-on involvement.

Tip: Be specific about your responsibilities. Avoid general statements and focus on concrete tasks that show your active role.

2. Organizational Chart

An organizational chart can help demonstrate your role in managing the business. If you're hiring staff, include an org chart that shows your position at the top, with other key roles beneath you. This visual helps USCIS see that you're the primary decision-maker.

Tip: Even if your team is small, an org chart showing your role relative to employees or contractors can be valuable. It clarifies your management position.

3. Business Plans and Meeting Minutes

Your business plan is another opportunity to show your intent to direct the business. Include details about your goals, growth plans, and expansion strategies to demonstrate that you're actively planning and leading the business. For ongoing proof, keep records of key meetings and decisions.

Anecdote: Using a Business Plan to Document Leadership

An E-2 investor from the UK included a detailed business plan for his real estate business, outlining monthly goals, hiring projections, and expansion plans for the next five years. USCIS appreciated the comprehensive approach, as it clearly showed his intention to develop and lead the business.

Tip: After submitting your application, maintain a habit of documenting meetings and decisions. This can be useful if you need to renew your visa or show proof of ongoing management.

Bringing It All Together

Compiling documentation for an E-2 visa may feel daunting, but with a checklist and a little organization, it's entirely manageable. By carefully assembling your financial evidence, business documents, and proof of active involvement, you can build a strong case for your E-2 application.

Remember, thoroughness is key—USCIS wants a complete, clear picture of your business and your role within it. Take the time to gather and present each document carefully, and your well-prepared application will be that much closer to approval.

CHAPTER 7: PREPARING FOR AND NAVIGATING THE E-2 VISA INTERVIEW

By the time you reach the E-2 visa interview, you've already poured significant time, energy, and resources into your application. Your business plan is finalized, documents are neatly compiled, and you're ready to take the last step: the interview. This can be the most nerve-wracking part of the process, but with preparation, you can walk into the interview room feeling confident and ready to present your case.

In this chapter, we'll break down what to expect during the E-2 visa interview, how to prepare your case, and ways to handle challenges if things don't go as planned. Think of this chapter as your guide to making a strong final impression and handling any unexpected hurdles.

What to Expect at the Interview: Location, Timelines, and Common Questions

The E-2 visa interview is typically held at a U.S. consulate or embassy in your home country, although in some cases, it may be possible to attend at another consulate location. This interview allows the consular officer to ask questions about your business, your role, and your plans in the U.S. It's their chance to verify that your investment is legitimate and that you meet all E-2 requirements.

1. Location and Timing of the Interview

The exact location of your interview depends on the U.S. consulate or embassy closest to you. Once you've submitted your application, you'll be given instructions on scheduling your interview. Keep in mind that consulate timelines vary depending on the location and the time of year, so be sure to check for any seasonal backlogs or wait times.

Example: Scheduling Delays During High-Demand Seasons

One E-2 investor from India found that summer was a particularly busy time for U.S. consulates, with longer-than-usual wait times. He planned his application submission in advance to avoid delays, making sure he had ample time to schedule his interview without cutting it too close to his intended start date in the U.S.

Tip: Plan your timeline carefully, and allow extra time for any unforeseen delays. If possible, avoid scheduling during peak times, like holiday seasons, when consulates are often busier.

2. Preparing for Common Interview Questions

During the interview, you'll likely be asked questions about your business, investment, and future plans. These questions aren't meant to trip you up but rather to confirm that you're fully committed to the business and understand the requirements of the E-2 visa. Here are some common questions and tips for answering them:

- **"What does your business do?"** Be ready to give a brief overview of your business model. Keep it clear and concise, focusing on the primary products or services

you offer.
- **"Why did you choose this particular business?"** This question gives you an opportunity to discuss your passion, experience, or background in the industry. Make it personal and professional.
- **"How did you acquire the investment funds?"** Be prepared to explain the origin of your funds, showing that they're from legitimate sources. Briefly summarize your financial documentation if necessary.
- **"What role will you play in managing the business?"** Highlight your responsibilities and day-to-day involvement. This shows the consular officer that you're not just a passive investor but are actively managing the business.

Anecdote: A Smooth Response on Business Choice

An E-2 applicant from Japan was asked why she chose to open a spa. She responded by talking about her previous experience managing wellness centers in Tokyo and her love for the industry. This personal connection helped the consular officer see her genuine interest, which reinforced her commitment to the business.

Tip: Practice answering these questions with a friend or family member. The more comfortable you feel discussing your business, the more confident you'll come across in the interview.

3. Document Verification

In some cases, the consular officer may ask to see certain documents from your application. Bring all original documents, including proof of funds, your business plan, lease agreements, and any other critical documentation. Being able to quickly provide these documents demonstrates that you're well-prepared and organized.

Tip: Organize your documents in a folder with labeled tabs so you can easily find and present any document requested.

Preparing Your Case: Strategies to Present Your Investment and Commitment Clearly

A strong interview performance requires more than just answering questions. It's about confidently presenting your investment, showing that you're committed to actively managing your business, and demonstrating your genuine intentions for applying.

1. Understanding Your Business Inside and Out

To succeed in the interview, you need to know your business inside and out. Be prepared to discuss market conditions, competition, financial projections, and job creation goals. The consular officer doesn't expect you to know every detail by memory, but having a good understanding shows that you're serious about making the business a success.

Case Study: Knowing the Numbers

An E-2 investor from Germany who was opening a tech consulting firm had a consular officer ask him specific questions about his financial projections. Because he had thoroughly reviewed his business plan, he was able to confidently explain his revenue goals, anticipated expenses, and expected profit margins. His preparedness left a positive impression, and his visa was approved.

Tip: Review your business plan and financial projections before the interview. If you're not confident with financial details, practice explaining them to someone else to build familiarity.

2. Demonstrating Your Commitment and Active Role

The E-2 visa requires active management, so emphasize your commitment to being fully involved. Describe your responsibilities and provide examples of tasks you'll manage personally. Consular officers want to see that you're not just an investor but an engaged entrepreneur.

Anecdote: Detailing Day-to-Day Responsibilities

An E-2 applicant from Mexico applying to open a restaurant in Miami was asked about his daily responsibilities. He spoke about planning the menu, overseeing kitchen operations, hiring staff, and engaging with customers. This level of detail reinforced his active role, making it clear that he was fully committed to managing the restaurant.

Tip: Outline your specific duties and prepare to discuss them in detail. Showing that you're personally invested in the business's success can go a long way in establishing your credibility.

3. Preparing a Strong Personal Story

Personal stories can be powerful in an interview setting. Sharing why you're passionate about your business, or how your background aligns with the business idea, can humanize your application and help the consular officer see you as a genuine, committed individual.

Example: Personal Motivation in a Health and Wellness Business

One applicant opening a health and wellness center shared her own journey with health challenges and how that inspired her to help others. This personal connection helped the consular officer understand her commitment to the business and her desire to make a meaningful impact, adding strength to her application.

Tip: Think about why this business is meaningful to you and how it aligns with your personal values or goals. Sharing this can make your application feel more authentic and relatable.

Handling Challenges and Rejections: Understanding Reasons for Rejection, Re-Application Tips, and Resolving Common Issues

Despite your best efforts, sometimes the interview doesn't go as planned. If you face a challenge, remember that rejection isn't necessarily the end. There are ways to address issues, reapply, and even turn a "no" into a "yes."

1. Common Reasons for Rejection

Knowing why some E-2 applications are denied can help you avoid common pitfalls. Here are a few frequent reasons:

- **Insufficient Investment**: If the consular officer feels that your investment amount isn't substantial enough to support the business, they may deny your application. Ensure your investment amount aligns with industry norms and is adequate for your business type.
- **Unclear Source of Funds**: If your documentation doesn't clearly show the origin of your funds, the officer may question the legitimacy of your investment.
- **Lack of Active Role**: If you can't demonstrate active involvement in managing the business, USCIS may deny the application. Show that you're fully committed and directly involved in the business's day-to-day operations.

Case Study: Handling a Rejection Due to Insufficient Investment

An E-2 applicant from Brazil was initially rejected because the consular officer felt his investment was too low for his planned retail business. He took the feedback seriously, increased his investment, and provided additional financial documentation to prove the investment was sufficient. On his second attempt, he received approval.

Tip: Don't be discouraged by a rejection. Use any feedback you receive to strengthen your application and address weak points before reapplying.

2. Tips for Re-Application and Resolving Issues

If you're rejected, take a step back and carefully review the reasons provided by the consulate. Address each issue thoroughly in your re-application, and consider consulting an immigration attorney for guidance on strengthening your case.

- **Increase Your Investment**: If the issue was insufficient funds, consider adding more capital to your business or expanding your business plan to include additional expenses or goals.
- **Clarify Your Role**: If active management was a concern, adjust your business plan or include more details about your role, responsibilities, and daily tasks.

Example: Re-Applying with a Stronger Business Plan

An E-2 applicant from Australia had her application denied due to vague job creation goals. She revised her business plan, adding specific job descriptions, projected salaries, and hiring timelines. When she reapplied, her enhanced job creation plan helped her secure approval.

Tip: Address each issue in detail. Re-application shows persistence, and a well-prepared response can help turn the outcome in your favor.

3. Staying Calm and Professional During the Interview

If you encounter challenging questions, stay calm and remember that the consular officer isn't trying to catch you off guard —they just need reassurance that your application meets requirements. A calm, professional demeanor can go a long way in demonstrating your confidence and commitment.

Anecdote: Handling Tough Questions with Confidence

One E-2 investor from Italy was asked pointed questions about the competitive landscape of his tech start-up. Rather than getting flustered, he calmly explained how his software's unique features set him apart. His poise left a positive impression, and he later learned that his confidence had been a key factor in his approval.

Tip: If you don't know an answer, it's okay to say, "I don't have that information on hand, but I can provide additional documentation if needed." Honesty and professionalism are better than guessing or giving uncertain answers.

Bringing It All Together

The E-2 visa interview is your final opportunity to present your case, clarify your intentions, and show that you're fully committed to making your business a success in the United States. With preparation, confidence, and a solid understanding of your business, you can handle the interview with ease and make a strong impression on the consular officer.

Remember, if things don't go as planned, there's always a way to address issues and try again. By using the tips and strategies outlined in this chapter, you'll be ready to approach the interview with confidence and increase your chances of securing your E-2 visa.

CHAPTER 8: LEGAL AND COMPLIANCE REQUIREMENTS POST-APPROVAL

Getting approved for the E-2 visa is an incredible accomplishment. But after you celebrate this milestone, it's time to focus on ensuring your business complies with U.S. legal requirements, immigration standards, and E-2 visa conditions. Think of this phase as laying the foundation for your business's long-term success in the U.S.

This chapter will walk you through the essential steps to form your business legally, maintain compliance with E-2 immigration regulations, and meet job creation mandates. With these bases covered, you'll be in a solid position to keep your visa in good standing, allowing you to focus on growing your business and enjoying your life in the U.S.

Forming Your U.S. Business Legally: Registering the Business, Acquiring Licenses, and Meeting Local Requirements

Setting up your business legally is the first step after receiving E-2 approval. You'll need to complete the business registration process, acquire any required licenses, and meet state or local compliance regulations. These steps are critical to operate your business without disruptions, and they demonstrate to USCIS that your business is legitimate and compliant.

1. Registering Your Business

The first legal step is to register your business in the state where you'll operate. Each state has its own registration process, so it's essential to familiarize yourself with the requirements in your chosen state.

- **Choose a Business Structure**: Most E-2 investors set up their businesses as an LLC (Limited Liability Company) or corporation. Both structures offer liability protection, but they come with different tax obligations and management requirements.
- **File Formation Documents**: Once you've chosen your structure, file the necessary formation documents with your state. For an LLC, you'll file Articles of Organization, while corporations file Articles of Incorporation. This process officially establishes your business with the state.
- **Get an Employer Identification Number (EIN)**: The EIN, issued by the IRS, is essential for tax purposes, opening a business bank account, and hiring employees. It's like a social security number for your business.

Example: Registering an LLC for a Consulting Firm

An E-2 investor from the UK who started a consulting firm in Texas chose to form an LLC to keep her business structure simple and flexible. She filed her Articles of Organization with the Texas Secretary of State and obtained an EIN. With these documents in place, she was ready to open a business bank account and start operations.

Tip: Many states have online portals for business registration, making it easy to file documents. If you're unsure about which business structure to choose, consulting a tax advisor or attorney can help you make the best choice.

2. Acquiring Required Licenses and Permits

Business licenses and permits vary widely depending on your industry and location. Some industries, such as hospitality or health services, have specific licensing requirements, while others may only require a general business license. Here are common types of licenses you might need:

- **General Business License**: Many cities or counties require a basic business license to operate within their jurisdiction.
- **Industry-Specific Permits**: If you're in a regulated industry, like food service, you may need additional permits, such as health and safety permits, alcohol licenses, or specialized certifications.
- **Zoning Permits**: Check local zoning regulations, especially if you're running a physical location. Zoning laws can restrict certain types of businesses in residential areas or require additional permits for modifications.

Case Study: Getting a Health Permit for a Café

An E-2 investor from Argentina opened a café in Los Angeles. Beyond her business license, she needed a health permit from the county health department, as well as a food handling certification for herself and her employees. She carefully completed each licensing requirement to ensure her café complied with all health regulations, setting her up for a smooth opening.

Tip: Contact your local city or county office to confirm which licenses you'll need. Many licensing requirements are industry-specific, so gathering the right information is crucial to avoid unexpected delays.

3. Meeting State and Local Compliance Requirements

State and local governments have additional regulations for businesses, such as state taxes, sales tax permits, and record-keeping requirements. Staying on top of these requirements helps you avoid fines and demonstrates your commitment to operating a legitimate, law-abiding business.

Tip: Set reminders for important deadlines, such as annual report filings or license renewals. Staying proactive can help you avoid late fees and keep your business in good standing.

Immigration Compliance for E-2 Investors: Requirements for Maintaining E-2 Status

Maintaining your E-2 status goes beyond starting your business. USCIS requires that you stay actively involved in managing the business and demonstrate its ongoing viability. Immigration compliance is critical to ensure smooth renewals and avoid jeopardizing your visa.

1. Staying Actively Involved in Business Operations

As an E-2 visa holder, you need to remain actively involved in the day-to-day management of your business. This requirement reinforces USCIS's expectation that E-2 investors are more than passive shareholders—they're hands-on leaders in their enterprise.

Anecdote: Staying Actively Involved in a Fitness Center

An E-2 investor from Japan opened a boutique fitness center in New York City. He was involved in almost every aspect, from scheduling classes to managing marketing. His daily engagement in the business helped him establish a strong record of active management, which made his visa renewal process smooth.

Tip: Document your involvement in business operations. Keeping meeting notes, business plans, and strategy updates can serve as proof of your active role if needed for visa renewals.

2. Keeping Detailed Financial Records

USCIS wants to see that your business is financially viable. This means maintaining detailed financial records, including profit and loss statements, tax returns, and bank statements. Strong financial documentation helps establish that your business is sustainable and supporting the local economy.

Example: Using Financial Records to Strengthen an Application

An E-2 investor from Mexico who owned a small retail shop in Texas kept monthly profit and loss statements, annual tax returns, and bank statements. When it came time to renew her visa, these records helped show that her business was profitable and contributing to the local economy, which was essential for her renewal approval.

Tip: Regularly update your financial records. Monthly financial reviews can keep you informed about your business's health and make it easier to provide documentation during renewals.

3. Adhering to Visa Conditions and Notifying USCIS of Major Changes

If there are significant changes in your business—such as ownership, structure, or location—you may need to notify USCIS. Changes in your business may impact your E-2 status, so keeping USCIS informed ensures you remain compliant.

Example: Relocating a Business and Informing USCIS

An E-2 investor from Italy who owned a consulting business relocated her office from Los Angeles to San Francisco. Before the move, she contacted USCIS to confirm whether her visa would be affected by the change. Keeping USCIS in the loop helped her avoid any misunderstandings and kept her visa in good standing.

Tip: If you're planning a major change, consult with an immigration attorney to understand how it might impact your E-2 status. Being proactive can help you avoid potential compliance issues.

Employee and Job Creation Mandates: Hiring U.S. Employees and Creating Jobs to Meet Visa Renewal Criteria

Creating jobs for U.S. workers is a key expectation of the E-2 visa. Demonstrating that your business supports local employment is important for your visa renewal, and it's also a great way to strengthen your ties to the community.

1. Setting Realistic Job Creation Goals

One of the E-2 visa's goals is economic contribution, which includes hiring U.S. employees. While there's no set minimum number of jobs required, USCIS wants to see that your business is creating a positive impact on the local job market.

Example: Planning Job Creation in a Restaurant

An E-2 investor from Canada opened a restaurant in Chicago. In her business plan, she outlined a hiring schedule: kitchen staff and waitstaff in the first six months, followed by a manager in year two as the restaurant expanded. By planning job creation in stages, she balanced her budget while meeting E-2 requirements.

Tip: Start with a realistic hiring plan that aligns with your business's growth. Even a few part-time roles can demonstrate job creation and economic impact.

2. Ensuring Compliance with U.S. Labor Laws

Hiring employees means complying with U.S. labor laws,

including paying at least minimum wage, offering a safe work environment, and following state employment regulations. Compliance with labor laws is crucial to maintaining a positive work culture and protecting your E-2 status.

Case Study: Hiring Responsibly for a Landscaping Business

An E-2 investor from Ireland who started a landscaping business in Florida made sure to comply with federal and state wage laws. By offering fair wages and a safe work environment, he not only complied with labor laws but also created a positive reputation in the community, helping his business grow.

Tip: Familiarize yourself with labor laws in your state. Compliance is key, and following best practices can also boost employee satisfaction and retention.

3. Documenting Job Creation for Visa Renewal

When renewing your E-2 visa, you'll need to show evidence of job creation and business contributions to the economy. Documentation should include employee tax forms (W-2s), payroll records, and job descriptions.

Anecdote: Using Payroll Records for Renewal

An E-2 investor from France who owned a retail store in Austin, Texas, carefully documented each employee's job title, wages, and work hours. When she applied for her visa renewal, this organized recordkeeping demonstrated her commitment to job creation, making her application process smoother.

Tip: Keep payroll and employee records organized and accessible. Having clear documentation of your job creation efforts will make the renewal process easier.

Bringing It All Together

Once your E-2 visa is approved, the journey is just beginning. Setting up your business legally, adhering to immigration compliance standards, and creating jobs are essential parts of running a successful business and maintaining your E-2 status. By staying proactive, organized, and informed, you'll not only strengthen your business's foundation but also set yourself up for successful visa renewals.

Remember, the work you put into legal and compliance requirements now will pay off by keeping your business—and your visa—in good standing. Approach each step with care, and you'll be well-positioned to make the most of your E-2 experience in the United States.

Part 4: Building and Growing Your E-2 Business

CHAPTER 9: SETTING UP YOUR BUSINESS OPERATIONS IN THE U.S.

Once your E-2 visa is approved and you're ready to bring your business vision to life, the real adventure begins. Now it's time to set up operations in a new country, with different market dynamics, cultural norms, and legal requirements. This can be a daunting task, but it's also incredibly rewarding as you lay the foundation for your business to thrive in the U.S.

In this chapter, we'll explore the essentials of setting up your business operations, from establishing a physical and online presence to navigating hiring practices and managing U.S. tax requirements. With a mix of practical advice and real-life examples, this guide will help you start strong as you take on the U.S. market.

Establishing Physical and Online Presence: Office Setup, Digital Presence, and Branding for U.S. Markets

Creating a physical and online presence is the first big step to making your business known in the U.S. Whether you're opening a storefront, setting up an office, or creating an e-commerce brand, building visibility is essential to attracting customers and establishing credibility.

1. Choosing the Right Physical Location

For some businesses, a physical location is essential, while others may benefit from a remote setup or shared office space. Choosing the right setup depends on your business needs, target audience, and budget.

- **Office or Storefront**: For retail, hospitality, or customer-facing services, a dedicated physical space is key. Choose a location that's accessible to your target audience, whether it's a bustling shopping district, a trendy neighborhood, or a convenient office complex.
- **Co-Working Spaces**: If you're a service-based or remote-friendly business, co-working spaces offer flexible, professional environments without the high overhead of traditional leases. Many co-working spaces also provide networking opportunities with other small businesses and startups.
- **Home Office**: Some entrepreneurs operate from home to save on overhead. If this is the case, make sure you have a dedicated workspace that's comfortable and conducive to productivity.

Example: Choosing a Storefront for a Boutique

An E-2 investor from France opened a boutique clothing store in San Francisco. She chose a small storefront in a popular shopping district, even though the rent was higher than in other areas. The location paid off, as foot traffic helped establish her brand quickly and attract a loyal customer base. She also ensured the store's design matched her brand's aesthetic, creating a memorable shopping experience.

Tip: Invest time in researching locations. Even if your business isn't customer-facing, being part of a supportive or like-minded community can positively impact your growth.

2. Building an Online Presence

In today's digital age, having an online presence is essential for all businesses, whether you're selling online or running a physical store. Your online presence is your chance to connect with a broader audience and communicate your brand message.

- **Website**: A professional, easy-to-navigate website is crucial. Make sure it's mobile-friendly, as a significant portion of customers will likely visit from their phones. Include essential information like business hours, contact details, and an overview of your products or services.
- **Social Media**: Choose platforms where your target audience is most active. Instagram, Facebook, and LinkedIn are popular for businesses, but explore other options if they fit your industry, such as Pinterest for lifestyle brands or TikTok for younger audiences.
- **Google Business Profile**: Claiming and optimizing your Google Business Profile helps customers find you on Google Maps and search results. This is particularly important for local businesses that rely on foot traffic.

Anecdote: Social Media Success for a Small Restaurant

An E-2 investor from Japan opened a ramen shop in Los Angeles and quickly built an Instagram following by posting mouth-watering photos of his dishes and stories about each recipe's origins. His Instagram page attracted customers before the restaurant even opened, and many came specifically because they saw his posts. This online presence helped the restaurant hit the ground running and reach a broader audience.

Tip: Consistency is key to building an online presence. Post regularly, engage with followers, and provide content that reflects your brand values and resonates with your audience.

3. Crafting a Brand That Speaks to U.S. Customers

Adapting your branding to appeal to U.S. customers is essential for making an impact. Your brand identity should resonate with the values, preferences, and cultural nuances of your target audience.

- **Messaging**: Tailor your brand messaging to U.S. market preferences. For example, Americans tend to respond well to authenticity, storytelling, and value-driven brands.
- **Visuals**: The U.S. market is diverse, but certain visual trends resonate widely, such as modern, minimalist design or warm, inviting aesthetics.
- **Customer Service**: U.S. consumers often expect a high level of customer service, so consider how you can go above and beyond. Positive experiences lead to customer loyalty and word-of-mouth referrals.

Example: Adapting a European Brand for U.S. Tastes

An E-2 investor from Italy started a bakery in New York City. While she initially planned to replicate her European branding, she adapted her approach by emphasizing American flavors, offering loyalty programs, and creating a warm, welcoming atmosphere that appealed to local tastes. This flexibility helped her bakery build a strong customer base.

Tip: Observe successful local businesses and note the elements they use in branding, messaging, and customer interaction. Incorporating these insights can help you better connect with U.S. consumers.

Hiring and Workforce Management: Understanding U.S. Labor Laws and Building a Productive Team

Hiring the right team can be transformative for your business, especially in a new market. U.S. labor laws have specific requirements that may be different from what you're used to, so understanding these is essential for compliance and for building a motivated team.

1. Navigating U.S. Labor Laws

U.S. labor laws cover everything from minimum wage to work hours and employee rights. Compliance is critical to avoid legal issues and maintain a positive work environment.

- **Minimum Wage and Overtime**: Each state has its own minimum wage, which may be higher than the federal minimum wage. If employees work over 40 hours a week, they're typically entitled to overtime pay.
- **Worker Classification**: Employees and contractors are classified differently. Contractors generally have more independence and aren't entitled to benefits, but misclassifying employees can lead to penalties.
- **Safety Regulations**: The Occupational Safety and Health Administration (OSHA) requires employers to provide a safe workplace. Be sure to comply with all relevant safety standards, especially if you're in an industry like construction or manufacturing.

Case Study: Navigating Compliance for a Small Manufacturing Business

An E-2 investor from Germany who opened a small manufacturing shop in North Carolina learned the importance of OSHA regulations early on. He invested in proper safety training and equipment, which helped prevent workplace accidents and ensured his business stayed compliant with U.S. safety standards.

Tip: Consult with a local labor attorney or HR specialist to understand the specific labor laws in your state. Compliance is critical, but it can also build trust with your employees.

2. Building a Strong Team

A great team is at the heart of every successful business. When hiring in the U.S., consider not only qualifications but also cultural fit and enthusiasm for your business's mission.

- **Recruiting Local Talent**: Post jobs on platforms like Indeed, LinkedIn, and local job boards. Networking in your community can also help you find potential hires who align with your business values.
- **Onboarding**: Take time to train your employees. Clear expectations and strong training set the foundation for a positive work culture.
- **Employee Retention**: Competitive wages, benefits, and growth opportunities are essential to keeping your team engaged. Small perks like team lunches, flexible schedules, or professional development opportunities can also make a big difference.

Anecdote: Building a Loyal Team at a Family-Owned Restaurant

An E-2 investor from South Korea opened a family-style restaurant in Seattle. She focused on creating a warm, inclusive environment for her employees by offering training, regular team meetings, and open communication. Her approach helped build a loyal, motivated team that felt like family, which translated into excellent service and customer satisfaction.

Tip: Foster an open-door policy with employees. A supportive work culture can boost productivity, reduce turnover, and make your business a more enjoyable place to work.

3. Managing Payroll and Benefits

Paying employees properly is essential for compliance and employee satisfaction. U.S. payroll involves taxes, Social Security, and sometimes additional benefits, which can vary based on location and company size.

- **Payroll Taxes**: Employers must withhold federal and state income taxes from employee wages, along with Social Security and Medicare taxes. Working with a payroll service can simplify this process.
- **Employee Benefits**: While not all small businesses offer benefits, health insurance, paid time off, and

retirement plans are attractive options if your budget allows.
- **Time Tracking**: For hourly employees, it's essential to track time accurately. Many businesses use time-tracking software to ensure compliance with overtime regulations.

Example: Setting Up Payroll for a Small Design Firm

An E-2 investor from Canada hired a payroll company to handle her design firm's payroll, tax withholdings, and benefits. This allowed her to focus on growing the business while ensuring her team was paid on time and in compliance with tax laws.

Tip: Consider using a payroll service to manage pay, taxes, and benefits. This can save you time, reduce errors, and ensure compliance with U.S. labor laws.

Financial and Tax Considerations: Accounting Practices, U.S. Tax Requirements, and Financial Management

Managing your finances is essential for both business success and compliance with U.S. tax laws. Establishing sound financial practices from the beginning can help you track your business's health, plan for growth, and avoid any surprises during tax season.

1. Establishing an Accounting System

Good accounting practices are the backbone of a well-managed business. Setting up an accounting system early will make tracking revenue, expenses, and profits much easier.

- **Accounting Software**: Many small businesses use software like QuickBooks, Xero, or FreshBooks to manage accounting tasks. These platforms simplify tracking expenses, sending invoices, and preparing for tax season.

- **Bookkeeping**: Consistent bookkeeping helps you stay on top of your finances. Either hire a part-time bookkeeper or dedicate time each week to recording transactions, managing invoices, and reconciling accounts.
- **Budgeting and Cash Flow**: Create a monthly budget and monitor cash flow regularly. Knowing your financial position allows you to make informed decisions, invest in growth, and manage unexpected expenses.

Tip: If you're new to U.S. accounting practices, consider hiring a part-time accountant or bookkeeper to guide you during the initial stages.

2. Understanding U.S. Tax Requirements

The U.S. tax system includes federal, state, and sometimes local taxes, and compliance is critical for maintaining good standing.

- **Income Taxes**: Businesses are generally required to pay federal income tax and, depending on the state, state income tax as well.
- **Sales Tax**: If you're selling products, you'll likely need to collect and remit sales tax. Each state has different sales tax rules, so check your local regulations.
- **Estimated Taxes**: Unlike salaried employees, business owners often need to make quarterly estimated tax payments to avoid penalties. Your accountant or tax advisor can help calculate these payments.

Example: Managing Sales Tax for an E-Commerce Business

An E-2 investor from India who started an e-commerce business learned that she needed to collect sales tax in certain states due to "economic nexus" laws. She used an e-commerce platform with built-in tax calculation features to simplify the process, ensuring compliance with state requirements.

Tip: Tax laws vary widely across states, so consult a tax advisor familiar with your industry and location to ensure you're meeting all obligations.

3. Financial Management and Planning for Growth

Planning for growth requires a proactive approach to financial management. Regularly review your financial statements and seek opportunities to optimize spending, increase revenue, and invest in areas that will drive growth.

- **Financial Statements**: Review your income statement, balance sheet, and cash flow statement each month. These reports provide insights into your business's health and help you make informed decisions.
- **Expense Tracking**: Categorize expenses and look for areas to save money without compromising quality. Even small adjustments can improve your bottom line.
- **Investing in Growth**: As your business stabilizes, consider reinvesting profits into new products, technology, or additional locations.

Anecdote: Planning for Growth in a Wellness Center

An E-2 investor from Brazil opened a wellness center in Los Angeles. After a successful first year, she reinvested her profits into adding new services and expanding her online presence. Her careful financial management allowed her to grow sustainably without taking on debt.

Tip: Regularly review and adjust your financial plan. A proactive approach to financial management can help you seize growth opportunities while keeping your business stable.

Bringing It All Together

Setting up your business operations in the U.S. involves more than just opening your doors; it's about creating a solid foundation for success. From establishing a presence and hiring the right team to managing finances and taxes, these operational steps are key to a sustainable, compliant, and thriving business.

Taking the time to build a strong presence, hire thoughtfully, and manage finances responsibly will set you on the path to success in the U.S. market. With these elements in place, you'll be well-prepared to make your mark in your industry and enjoy the rewards of your hard work.

CHAPTER 10: MARKETING AND EXPANDING YOUR E-2 BUSINESS

Once your E-2 business is up and running, the next challenge is to spread the word and attract customers. The U.S. market is diverse, with consumers who are used to a variety of options and high standards for customer experience. Your marketing strategy is your chance to make your business stand out, create a loyal customer base, and expand over time.

In this chapter, we'll explore how to craft a marketing strategy tailored to the U.S. market, leverage networking opportunities, and build your brand through digital marketing. With practical examples, anecdotes, and tips, you'll be ready to promote your business in ways that resonate with American customers.

Crafting a U.S.-Focused Marketing Strategy: Identifying Target Markets, Creating Offers, and Engaging Customers

Creating a marketing strategy tailored to the U.S. market is essential. American consumers value authenticity, transparency, and quality, but they also respond well to compelling offers, clear communication, and personalized experiences.

1. Identifying Your Target Market

Defining your target audience helps you focus your efforts on reaching the people who are most likely to become loyal customers. Factors to consider include age, lifestyle, location, and purchasing habits. For example, if you're opening a vegan restaurant in Los Angeles, your target audience may include health-conscious millennials, whereas a tech consulting firm may target small business owners and start-ups.

Case Study: Targeting Young Professionals for a Coffee Shop

An E-2 investor from Colombia opened a coffee shop in a busy business district in Seattle. She targeted young professionals by offering a sleek, modern atmosphere with free Wi-Fi and comfortable seating, knowing these features would appeal to remote workers and on-the-go professionals. Her marketing included posters in nearby offices and a loyalty program that rewarded repeat visits. By focusing on this target audience, she quickly built a base of loyal customers who appreciated the shop's ambiance and convenience.

Tip: Create customer personas that describe the characteristics of your ideal customers. Personas can help you stay focused and develop offers that speak to specific audiences.

2. Creating Offers That Resonate

In the U.S., consumers are often drawn to special offers, introductory deals, and loyalty programs. These incentives can attract new customers and encourage repeat business, especially if you're in a competitive industry.

- **Introductory Offers**: Discounts for first-time customers or free samples work well for businesses looking to gain traction. A beauty salon might offer

a discount on the first visit, while a restaurant could promote a free appetizer or dessert for new customers.
- **Loyalty Programs**: Americans love loyalty rewards, from punch cards to points-based systems. A café could offer a free coffee after ten purchases, while a retail store might use an app to track points.
- **Seasonal Promotions**: Seasonal deals, like holiday sales or back-to-school specials, can drive traffic during specific times of the year. These are especially useful for retail businesses, restaurants, and online stores.

Example: Using a Loyalty Program for a Clothing Boutique

An E-2 investor from South Korea started a boutique in San Francisco, where she launched a loyalty program offering a 10% discount after five visits. This simple incentive encouraged shoppers to come back, and her customers enjoyed feeling rewarded. The program helped her build a steady customer base, especially among local fashion enthusiasts.

Tip: Experiment with different offers to see what works best for your audience. Track the results to see which promotions bring in the most business and repeat customers.

3. Engaging Customers with Great Service

In the U.S., customer service can make or break a business. Going above and beyond to make customers feel valued and appreciated not only helps build loyalty but also boosts word-of-mouth marketing, which is invaluable in the American market.

Anecdote: Winning Over Customers with Personalized Service

An E-2 investor from France who opened a bakery in New York City made a habit of chatting with her customers, remembering their favorite pastries, and even offering to save popular items for regulars. Her warm approach not only made customers feel valued but also led to enthusiastic online reviews, which helped attract even more customers.

Tip: Train your team to prioritize customer satisfaction. A simple, genuine interaction can leave a lasting impression, and happy customers are more likely to leave positive reviews and recommend your business to friends.

Networking and Building Partnerships: Leveraging Local Business Networks for Growth

Networking and partnerships are powerful tools for growing your business and building local credibility. By connecting with other business owners, organizations, and potential customers, you'll create valuable relationships that can lead to referrals, collaborations, and increased visibility.

1. Joining Local Business Networks

Joining a business network or chamber of commerce can introduce you to other entrepreneurs and potential clients. Many cities have organizations specifically designed to support small businesses, offering resources like networking events, workshops, and mentorship programs.

Case Study: Building a Network for a Health and Wellness Center

An E-2 investor from Brazil opened a wellness center in Miami. She joined the local chamber of commerce and attended health and wellness expos, where she met other business owners, local health professionals, and community leaders. These connections led to partnerships with nearby gyms and yoga studios, which helped her attract new clients.

Tip: Attend local networking events and join relevant associations. Building these relationships can open doors to partnerships, advice, and visibility in the community.

2. Collaborating with Complementary Businesses

Collaborating with other businesses can be a win-win for both parties, helping you reach new audiences and share resources. Look for businesses that complement yours but aren't direct competitors. For example, a spa could partner with a local hair salon to offer package deals, or a restaurant could team up with a nearby movie theater for a "dinner and a movie" promotion.

Example: Cross-Promotion with a Gym and Juice Bar

An E-2 investor from the UK who opened a juice bar in Los Angeles teamed up with a nearby gym to offer discounts to gym members. Gym-goers received a discount on smoothies, while juice bar customers got a free one-day pass to the gym. This cross-promotion drove traffic to both businesses and created mutual benefits.

Tip: Look for businesses with similar target audiences but different offerings. Cross-promotions can be a cost-effective way to expand your reach and build relationships with other business owners.

3. Attending Trade Shows and Industry Events

Trade shows and industry events offer networking opportunities, especially if your business is in a specialized field. These events can help you stay updated on industry trends, meet potential collaborators, and gain visibility.

Anecdote: Expanding a Tech Start-Up Through Trade Shows

An E-2 investor from India who launched a tech start-up in San Francisco attended a technology expo to introduce his product. He not only met potential clients but also connected with industry experts and investors. This experience helped him refine his product, build credibility, and secure partnerships.

Tip: Bring business cards, samples, or promotional materials to events. Follow up with new contacts afterward to keep the momentum going and build strong, lasting connections.

Digital Marketing Essentials: Utilizing Social Media, Email Marketing, and SEO for Visibility and Brand-Building

Digital marketing is essential for reaching a wide audience and building your brand online. With the right tools, you can connect with customers, drive traffic, and establish your business's presence in the U.S. market.

1. Social Media Marketing

Social media platforms like Instagram, Facebook, and LinkedIn are powerful tools for reaching customers, promoting products, and building brand loyalty. Each platform has its strengths, so focus on those that best fit your business and target audience.

- **Instagram**: Ideal for visually appealing products like food, fashion, and lifestyle brands. Share photos, stories, and reels to engage with followers.
- **Facebook**: Great for local businesses looking to connect with a community. Use Facebook to share updates, run ads, and communicate directly with customers.
- **LinkedIn**: Perfect for B2B companies, professional services, and networking. Post industry insights, share success stories, and connect with potential clients or partners.

Case Study: Growing a Café with Instagram

An E-2 investor from Japan opened a café in Austin, Texas, and used Instagram to attract foodies by posting mouth-watering photos of her unique Japanese-style pastries. By tagging her location, using relevant hashtags, and collaborating with local influencers, she quickly built a following, which translated to more customers in her café.

Tip: Use a content calendar to plan social media posts in advance.

Consistent, well-timed posts help keep your brand visible and engaging.

2. Email Marketing for Customer Engagement

Email marketing allows you to reach customers directly, whether you're sending special offers, product updates, or event invitations. A well-crafted email list can help you maintain customer relationships and encourage repeat business.

Example: Using Email to Promote Seasonal Offers in a Spa

An E-2 investor from Brazil who owned a day spa in Miami used email marketing to promote seasonal packages, like a Valentine's Day couples' package or a summer skincare special. These targeted offers encouraged customers to book appointments, increasing revenue during specific times of the year.

Tip: Segment your email list to send relevant offers to different types of customers. For example, loyal customers could receive VIP discounts, while new subscribers get introductory offers.

3. Search Engine Optimization (SEO) for Online Visibility

SEO helps your website rank higher in search engine results, making it easier for customers to find you. Optimizing your website for relevant keywords, creating quality content, and building backlinks are key components of a strong SEO strategy.

Anecdote: Improving SEO for a Niche Market

An E-2 investor from Canada opened a pet grooming business in Denver. By optimizing her website with keywords like "Denver pet grooming" and "cat grooming in Denver," she started to rank higher on Google, attracting more local pet owners. Her SEO strategy brought in a steady stream of clients who found her business through online searches.

Tip: Use tools like Google Analytics and Google Search Console to track your website's performance and refine your SEO strategy. Regularly update your website with fresh content to keep it relevant and engaging.

Bringing It All Together

Marketing and expanding your E-2 business in the U.S. is a journey that requires creativity, persistence, and adaptability. By building a strong, U.S.-focused marketing strategy, networking strategically, and harnessing digital tools, you'll be well-equipped to attract customers, build your brand, and grow your business.

Remember, the U.S. market is highly competitive, but it's also full of opportunities for those who are ready to innovate, connect, and engage with their audience. By following the tips and strategies in this chapter, you'll be on your way to creating a successful and sustainable business in the U.S.

Part 5: Maintaining and Renewing Your E-2 Visa

CHAPTER 11: PREPARING FOR E-2 VISA RENEWAL

Getting your E-2 visa was an achievement, but if you plan to stay and grow your business in the U.S., renewal will be on the horizon. The E-2 visa doesn't directly lead to permanent residency, so keeping your visa status active is essential if you want to remain in the U.S. as an investor. This process requires demonstrating that your business is still viable, profitable, and contributing to the local economy. Renewal can feel intimidating, but with the right approach, you can set yourself up for a smooth experience.

In this chapter, we'll explore the requirements for E-2 renewal, discuss strategies for ensuring business stability, and cover the documentation you'll need to prove your business's success. With careful preparation and consistent attention to your business, you'll be ready to make a strong case for renewal and continue thriving in the U.S.

Renewal Requirements: What USCIS Looks for in Renewals, Including Sustained Investment and Business Activity

When it's time to renew your E-2 visa, USCIS will look for evidence that your business is still a viable and active operation. They want to see that you're meeting the commitments made in your initial application, such as active management, continued investment, and job creation. Here's what they'll focus on:

1. Sustained Investment

USCIS wants to see that you're continuing to invest in your business, not just financially but with time, energy, and resources. Your business should demonstrate steady or increasing value, with assets and revenue that show you're serious about growth and profitability. While you don't have to keep pouring money in, showing that you've invested in growth initiatives, technology, or expanded services can work in your favor.

Example: Expanding Investment for a Fitness Center

An E-2 investor from Brazil started a fitness center in Houston with an initial investment in equipment and marketing. When it came time for renewal, he had invested in new classes, additional trainers, and upgraded facilities. These investments helped him show USCIS that he was committed to the business's long-term success and that it was steadily growing.

Tip: Plan for small, strategic reinvestments over time. Regular updates to equipment, new hires, or enhanced services demonstrate that you're actively working to keep the business competitive.

2. Business Activity and Profitability

Your business doesn't have to be a massive success, but USCIS expects to see signs of stability and growth. A steady revenue stream, customer base, and proof of demand for your products or services will go a long way in convincing them that your business is on the right track.

Case Study: Building a Steady Customer Base for a Café

An E-2 investor from Japan opened a small café in Portland. While he wasn't aiming to turn it into a national chain, his steady growth in revenue, consistent customer flow, and positive online reviews all helped build his case for renewal. He was able to show USCIS that his business was stable and had a solid foothold in the local community.

Tip: Keep track of metrics that reflect business activity, like monthly sales, customer growth, and online engagement. These indicators of demand and activity will strengthen your renewal application.

3. Job Creation and Economic Impact

One of the core purposes of the E-2 visa is to support economic growth in the U.S. by creating jobs for American workers. USCIS will look at your employee records and may also evaluate your business's indirect impact on the local economy.

Example: Job Creation for a Landscaping Business

An E-2 investor from Canada who owned a landscaping company in Florida steadily hired local workers as his business grew. By the time of his first renewal, he had four employees, demonstrating that his business was creating jobs and supporting the local economy. This growth helped him meet USCIS's job creation expectations, making his renewal process smoother.

Tip: If possible, outline a hiring plan from the beginning and keep track of each employee's contributions. Even a few part-time or seasonal positions can make a big difference in your renewal application.

Ensuring Business Stability and Growth: Strategies for Maintaining Profitability and Meeting Job Creation Expectations

To succeed in your renewal application, you'll need a business that not only operates smoothly but also shows signs of growth and stability. Here are a few strategies to keep your business on track and demonstrate ongoing success.

1. Focus on Consistent Revenue Streams

Consistent revenue is key to showing USCIS that your business is stable. Consider diversifying your offerings or adding subscription services, which can help ensure steady income. For instance, if you run a beauty salon, offering monthly memberships or package deals can provide predictable revenue and build customer loyalty.

Case Study: Implementing Subscriptions for a Pet Grooming Business

An E-2 investor from France who ran a pet grooming service in Chicago launched a monthly subscription for dog owners who wanted regular grooming services. This new revenue stream helped her business remain profitable year-round, even during slow seasons. Her steady income showed USCIS that her business was thriving and provided consistent value to her customers.

Tip: Review your revenue sources and explore opportunities to create regular income. Subscription models, memberships, and retainers work well in many industries and can help smooth out income fluctuations.

2. Maintaining a High Standard of Customer Service

U.S. consumers appreciate good service, and repeat customers can be a significant factor in business stability. Happy customers often bring referrals and positive reviews, which can make a noticeable impact on your revenue.

Anecdote: Building Loyalty with a Personal Touch

An E-2 investor from South Korea who owned a small family-style restaurant in San Diego focused on creating a welcoming environment. She greeted customers by name, offered personalized recommendations, and took time to chat. This level of care built a loyal customer base, which contributed to steady sales and favorable word-of-mouth that helped during her renewal process.

Tip: Encourage customer feedback and work continuously on improving service. Positive reviews and loyal customers can make a difference in showing USCIS the business's stability.

3. Staying Adaptable and Ready for Change

Flexibility is a valuable asset in maintaining a stable business. Market conditions change, and being open to adjusting your business model can keep you competitive. Evaluate industry trends, customer feedback, and performance data to make informed decisions on adapting your offerings.

Example: Pivoting Services in a Boutique

An E-2 investor from Italy opened a boutique clothing store in New York, initially focused on high-end fashion. After realizing her clientele was more interested in affordable, stylish pieces, she pivoted to offer a mix of affordable and designer clothing. This shift helped her reach a broader audience, increase revenue, and show USCIS that she could adapt to customer needs.

Tip: Regularly assess your business performance and be willing to make changes as needed. This flexibility can be a significant asset in demonstrating your business's resilience and growth potential.

Documenting and Proving Business Success: Financial Reports, Employee Records, and Updated Business Plans

Comprehensive documentation is key to proving your business's stability and success. USCIS will want to see tangible evidence that your business is active, financially healthy, and contributing to the local economy. Let's go over the essential records and documentation that can strengthen your renewal application.

1. Financial Reports

Strong financial documentation is critical for your renewal application. Profit and loss statements, balance sheets, and tax returns provide a clear picture of your business's financial health. Even if you're not a financial expert, keeping these documents organized is essential.

Example: Using Financial Reports to Show Growth in a Small Retail Shop

An E-2 investor from Japan who ran a retail shop in San Francisco kept monthly profit and loss statements, allowing her to track trends and demonstrate growth. When it came time for renewal, she was able to show that her revenue had increased by 15% each year, which impressed USCIS and made her renewal approval easier.

Tip: Work with an accountant to keep your financial records up to date. Regular reviews of your income, expenses, and profits make renewal applications smoother and help you make informed business decisions.

2. Employee Records

USCIS wants evidence of your business's economic impact, and employee records are a powerful way to demonstrate job creation. Maintain detailed records that include employee names, job titles, hire dates, and wages. If your business relies on seasonal or part-time workers, include documentation of these positions as well.

Case Study: Using Employee Records for a Landscaping Business Renewal

An E-2 investor from Canada, who ran a landscaping business in Texas, maintained clear records for his five full-time and seasonal employees. When he applied for renewal, these records helped him showcase his business's commitment to local employment and made a strong case for continued economic impact.

Tip: Organize employee records in a way that makes them easy to present. Payroll services can streamline record-keeping by providing clear, consistent reports on wages, hours, and taxes.

3. Updated Business Plans

An updated business plan can provide a clear overview of your growth, future goals, and strategies for ongoing success. It shows USCIS that you're not only managing the business effectively but are also planning for sustainable growth. Your plan should include projections, marketing strategies, and expansion ideas if relevant.

Anecdote: Updating a Business Plan for a Consulting Firm

An E-2 investor from the U.K. who owned a small consulting firm in Chicago used her renewal application as an opportunity to update her business plan. She included plans for expanding her services to a new market, which showed USCIS her commitment to growth. Her proactive approach demonstrated a forward-thinking business mindset, which helped her renewal application stand out.

Tip: Treat your business plan as a living document that you revisit and revise regularly. Highlight successes, challenges you've overcome, and your goals for the coming years.

4. Positive Customer Feedback and Online Presence

While not required, positive customer reviews and an active online presence can help demonstrate your business's reputation and engagement with the community. Websites, social media profiles, and Google reviews can support your case by showing that you have a steady, loyal customer base.

Example: Using Customer Reviews to Build Credibility for a Café

An E-2 investor from Argentina who owned a café in Miami included screenshots of online reviews as part of her renewal application. The glowing feedback from customers helped reinforce her business's popularity and stable income, which contributed to a successful renewal.

Tip: Encourage satisfied customers to leave reviews online. A strong online presence and positive feedback add credibility to your application and showcase your business's impact on the community.

Bringing It All Together

Preparing for your E-2 visa renewal might seem overwhelming, but with careful planning and thorough documentation, you can make the process smooth and stress-free. By consistently investing in your business, tracking its progress, and staying engaged with your customers and community, you'll be well-positioned to present a strong case to USCIS.

Remember, the key to a successful renewal is to show USCIS that your business is stable, growing, and contributing to the local economy. By following the tips and strategies in this chapter, you'll be ready to confidently submit your renewal application and continue building your E-2 business in the U.S.

CHAPTER 12: LONG-TERM STRATEGIES AND ALTERNATIVE RESIDENCY OPTIONS

When you start a business in the U.S. on an E-2 visa, you're taking on an exciting journey. But if you're thinking long-term, you might be wondering about your next steps. The E-2 visa is renewable but doesn't directly lead to permanent residency. Many E-2 investors eventually consider transitioning to a visa that provides a clearer path to a green card or exploring options that provide more stability for family members. Beyond visas, planning for business growth also becomes essential as you settle into the U.S. market.

In this chapter, we'll cover how to transition from the E-2 to the EB-5 or other visa options, explore alternative residency paths for you and your family, and discuss strategic business growth for the long haul. With a little planning and some insight into your options, you can chart a path that aligns with your long-term goals in the U.S.

Transitioning from E-2 to EB-5 or Other Visa Options: Overview of Possible Transitions to Permanent Residency

One of the most common questions E-2 investors ask is, "How can I eventually stay in the U.S. permanently?" The E-2 visa is fantastic for launching a business, but it has limitations if your goal is to live in the U.S. indefinitely. Fortunately, there are other visa options, like the EB-5, that offer a direct path to a green card.

1. Understanding the EB-5 Immigrant Investor Program

The EB-5 visa, known as the "Investor Green Card," is designed for foreign nationals who are willing to make a substantial investment in a U.S. business that creates jobs. While it requires a larger investment than the E-2, it offers permanent residency, which makes it appealing for investors looking for stability.

- **Investment Requirements**: As of now, the EB-5 visa requires an investment of $1.05 million, or $800,000 if the business is in a targeted employment area (TEA), such as rural regions or areas with high unemployment.
- **Job Creation Requirement**: The EB-5 visa mandates that your investment must create at least 10 full-time jobs for U.S. workers within two years. This job creation requirement is more specific and stringent than the E-2.
- **Direct vs. Regional Center Investments**: You can either invest directly in a business that you own and operate or go through a regional center, which pools investments for larger projects. Regional centers often handle job creation requirements for you, making it easier to meet EB-5 conditions.

Case Study: Transitioning from E-2 to EB-5 in a Restaurant Chain

An E-2 investor from South Korea who opened a successful restaurant in Los Angeles eventually transitioned to an EB-5 by expanding her business into a small chain with multiple locations. She reinvested her profits to meet the EB-5 minimum, and by creating jobs at each location, she met the job creation requirement. This transition allowed her to gain permanent residency without disrupting her business operations.

Tip: If you're considering the EB-5, start planning for it early. Think about how you can scale your business and create the necessary jobs to meet EB-5 requirements. Consulting with an immigration attorney experienced with the EB-5 process can be invaluable.

2. The EB-2 National Interest Waiver (NIW)

Another option is the EB-2 National Interest Waiver (NIW), which is suitable for individuals whose work can be shown to benefit the U.S. in a significant way. The EB-2 NIW is often pursued by entrepreneurs and investors with specialized skills, especially if their business aligns with national interests, such as technology, healthcare, or education.

- **No Specific Investment Requirement**: Unlike the EB-5, the EB-2 NIW does not require a specific investment amount. Instead, applicants must demonstrate that their work holds substantial merit and benefits the U.S.
- **Flexibility in Business Model**: The EB-2 NIW offers more flexibility because it focuses on the business's impact rather than investment size. If your business tackles a pressing issue or provides significant community benefits, this could be a viable path.

Example: Transitioning from E-2 to EB-2 NIW as a Tech Entrepreneur

An E-2 investor from India running a tech start-up in San Francisco applied for an EB-2 NIW by demonstrating how his company's innovative software contributed to cybersecurity —a priority for U.S. interests. By highlighting the national importance of his business, he successfully transitioned to an EB-2 NIW, securing his pathway to a green card.

Tip: If your business aligns with sectors that hold national importance, such as green energy or healthcare, explore the EB-2 NIW as an option. This visa is more flexible but does require a strong case and supporting evidence.

3. H-1B for Skilled Employees and Business Owners

If you're highly skilled in your field, the H-1B visa might be a viable alternative. While typically used by employers to hire skilled foreign workers, entrepreneurs can sometimes apply if they meet the qualifications and structure their business correctly. This visa requires a specific job offer and a role that requires specialized knowledge, such as engineering or computer science.

Tip: If you're considering the H-1B route, consult with an attorney to ensure your business structure and job role meet the H-1B criteria. This route has more specific requirements, but it can work for business owners in specialized fields.

Alternative Residency Paths: Options for Family Members, Possible Paths to Green Cards, and Navigating the Transition

If you're thinking about the future for your family, you'll want to explore options for them as well. The E-2 visa allows spouses and children under 21 to join you in the U.S., but you may want to consider alternative residency options to provide stability for your loved ones.

1. Employment Authorization for Spouses

One of the benefits of the E-2 visa is that spouses are eligible for work authorization, which allows them to work anywhere in the U.S., regardless of your business. This can be helpful if your spouse wants to build their own career or even start their own business.

Anecdote: Leveraging Spousal Employment Authorization

An E-2 investor from Canada opened a retail business in Florida, while his spouse, also Canadian, obtained employment authorization and started a freelance graphic design business. This not only supplemented their household income but also gave the family flexibility and security, especially during slower business periods.

Tip: Encourage your spouse to explore work options that align with their interests. This can diversify your family's income streams and build a broader network in the U.S.

2. Transitioning Children to Other Visas

Children on E-2 visas can only remain in the U.S. until they turn 21. After that, they'll need their own visa to stay in the country. Many families choose to transition children to student (F-1) visas if they're attending college, or they may explore work visas like the H-1B once they enter the workforce.

Example: Transitioning to an F-1 Visa for University

An E-2 investor from France whose son turned 21 transitioned him to an F-1 student visa when he started university. This allowed him to remain in the U.S. and eventually pursue a career there on his own visa, ensuring continuity for the entire family.

Tip: Start planning for your children's visa transition early. If they're interested in studying or working in the U.S., discuss potential visa options with an immigration attorney well before their 21st birthday.

3. Family Sponsorship as a Green Card Path

If you or your spouse has a family member who is a U.S. citizen or permanent resident, family sponsorship may be a potential green card path. This option may be especially useful if other visa transitions aren't feasible.

Tip: Keep family sponsorship as a backup option, especially if you're not ready to invest in an EB-5. Family sponsorship may take time but can provide a reliable route to permanent residency.

Strategic Business Growth: Planning for Long-Term Success Beyond E-2 Needs, Including Business Expansion and Diversification

While meeting the E-2 visa requirements is a priority, it's also essential to think beyond visa renewal. Building a long-term business strategy not only strengthens your visa case but also creates new opportunities, whether you choose to remain on the E-2 or transition to another visa.

1. Expanding Within Your Industry

Expansion can be a powerful way to grow your business and demonstrate commitment to the U.S. economy. Expanding within your industry can mean opening additional locations, launching new services, or developing partnerships.

Case Study: Expanding a Café Chain

An E-2 investor from Mexico opened a café in Austin, Texas, and over the years, expanded to three locations. By showing steady growth and increased job creation, she made a stronger case for her E-2 renewals and laid the groundwork for an eventual transition to the EB-5 visa.

Tip: Plan for gradual growth that aligns with your financial and staffing resources. Expansion doesn't have to be rapid, but each step forward strengthens your presence in the market.

2. Diversifying Your Offerings

Diversification helps protect your business from market

fluctuations and showcases your adaptability. If you're a restaurant owner, consider adding a catering service. If you run a retail store, look into e-commerce. These additional revenue streams make your business more resilient and demonstrate your commitment to long-term success.

Example: Adding Catering Services to a Restaurant

An E-2 investor from South Korea who owned a restaurant in San Francisco expanded into catering for events. This diversification provided additional revenue, especially during slower times for in-restaurant dining, and showcased her ability to adapt to changing market demands.

Tip: Look for complementary services or products that align with your brand. Diversification strengthens your business and can enhance your renewal application by showing sustainable growth.

3. Building Community Connections and Brand Loyalty

Establishing a strong brand and building connections with the local community can help your business thrive over the long term. Engage in local events, sponsor community initiatives, and cultivate brand loyalty by actively supporting the community you're in.

Anecdote: Building a Brand through Community Engagement

An E-2 investor from Italy who owned a boutique in New York City partnered with local artists to host events and feature their work. This not only created buzz around her business but also established her as an active and valued member of the community, boosting her brand's reputation.

Tip: Community engagement doesn't just help your business; it also strengthens your renewal application. USCIS appreciates seeing businesses that positively impact their local areas.

Bringing It All Together

The journey from E-2 visa holder to long-term resident requires careful planning, adaptability, and strategic thinking. Whether you're aiming for the EB-5, exploring options for family members, or focusing on long-term growth, there are multiple paths to achieve your goals.

By investing in your business, expanding strategically, and exploring visa transitions, you can build a future that aligns with both your personal and professional aspirations. Remember, every step you take to grow your business, build connections, and support your family brings you closer to a sustainable and fulfilling life in the U.S.

Part 6: Additional Resources and Case Studies

CHAPTER 13: COMMON PITFALLS AND HOW TO AVOID THEM

Starting a business in a new country is no small feat, and when it comes to E-2 visas, navigating the requirements and paperwork can feel like a balancing act. As an E-2 investor, you're juggling the responsibilities of managing a business, meeting visa conditions, and planning for long-term success. But like with any complex process, mistakes happen. This chapter dives into the common pitfalls E-2 investors face and offers practical advice on how to sidestep them.

From documentation errors and partnership issues to compliance challenges post-approval, we'll cover everything you need to know to keep your business and visa status secure. Avoiding these pitfalls can save you time, stress, and even the risk of visa denial.

Mistakes in Documentation: Avoiding Errors in Business Plans, Proof of Funds, and Applications

Documentation forms the backbone of your E-2 application. USCIS relies on a range of documents to assess your business's viability, your investment's legitimacy, and your qualifications as an investor. Even small errors can raise red flags or lead to delays. Here's a breakdown of common documentation mistakes and how to avoid them.

1. Overlooking Details in the Business Plan

The business plan is one of the most important documents in your E-2 application. It provides a roadmap for your business, detailing how you'll operate, attract customers, create jobs, and remain profitable. Common mistakes include vague market research, unrealistic financial projections, and lack of clarity around your active role.

Case Study: A Restaurant's Business Plan with Over-Optimistic Projections

An E-2 applicant from Brazil opened a restaurant in Miami and projected rapid revenue growth in her business plan, expecting a 50% increase each year. Her plan lacked detailed market research, making the growth projections seem unrealistic. USCIS flagged this as a concern, and she had to provide additional data, delaying her approval. In hindsight, a conservative and research-backed projection would have been more effective.

Tip: Base your projections on solid research. Aim for conservative, realistic growth and be prepared to back up your numbers with industry data. When it comes to financials, cautious realism is more convincing than optimistic guesswork.

2. Errors in Proof of Funds Documentation

Proving the source and legality of your funds is crucial for the E-2 visa. USCIS wants to see a clear, traceable path for your investment, but applicants often make mistakes by omitting key documents or failing to provide a complete paper trail.

- **Incomplete Documentation**: Include every document that shows where the funds came from, such as bank

statements, tax returns, or property sale records. Any gap in this paper trail could lead to delays.
- **Unclear Source of Funds**: If funds come from multiple sources, clearly organize and label each part of your documentation to show the exact path of your investment.

Example: Providing Clear Proof of Funds for a Tech Start-Up

An E-2 applicant from India faced issues when USCIS questioned his fund sources. After additional clarification and including detailed bank records, his funds were confirmed. This extra step could have been avoided by submitting clear, well-organized documentation from the start.

Tip: When it comes to proof of funds, think of your documentation as a story. Make it easy for USCIS to follow by organizing everything chronologically and labeling each part. The more straightforward the story, the easier it is for USCIS to approve your investment.

3. Double-Checking the Application for Accuracy

It may sound simple, but basic errors on the E-2 application form are surprisingly common. These mistakes often stem from rushing through the form, failing to double-check, or missing questions entirely.

Anecdote: Avoiding Simple Typos in an Application

An E-2 investor from France rushed through his application, accidentally transposing digits in his passport number. This small error triggered an additional review, delaying his approval. After correcting the issue, he made it a rule to triple-check every official form.

Tip: Take your time on the application and review every detail. It's a good idea to have a second set of eyes go over it. Small mistakes can lead to big delays.

Challenges with Partnerships and Compliance: Common Issues in Co-Investment Structures and Management Control

Many E-2 investors choose to go into business with a partner or join an existing company. While partnerships can be beneficial, they also introduce unique challenges, especially when it comes to E-2 requirements around active management and ownership.

1. Navigating Co-Investment Requirements

If you're going into business with a partner, ensuring that your ownership and control meet E-2 standards is critical. USCIS requires that E-2 investors have at least 50% ownership of the business or "operational control," so co-investing can be tricky.

Case Study: Partnership Control in a Retail Business

An E-2 investor from Canada partnered with a local entrepreneur to open a retail store in New York. They initially split ownership evenly, but USCIS flagged this as an issue. To resolve it, the E-2 investor adjusted his stake to 51% and clarified his control over key business decisions, which satisfied USCIS requirements.

Tip: Before finalizing a partnership, discuss and document decision-making roles. Consider maintaining at least 51% ownership or clearly define your managerial role to meet USCIS's control expectations.

2. Clarifying Roles in a Joint Venture

In joint ventures, roles can get blurred, which can lead to compliance issues. USCIS wants to see that E-2 investors are actively managing the business, so passive or silent partnerships may not qualify.

Example: Active Role in a Fitness Center Joint Venture

An E-2 investor from South Korea entered a joint venture to open a fitness center in California. Although he had a 50% share, he took on the day-to-day responsibilities of managing memberships, hiring trainers, and overseeing operations. USCIS appreciated his documented active role, which helped clarify his contribution.

Tip: Keep detailed records of your involvement and responsibilities. Monthly reports, meeting notes, and strategic plans can help demonstrate that you're actively engaged in running the business.

3. Avoiding Compliance Issues in Co-Management Structures

Co-managing a business can lead to compliance issues if roles aren't clearly defined. Ambiguity in responsibilities can make it harder for USCIS to see that you're fulfilling the "active management" requirement. Ensure your duties are outlined in writing and distinct from those of any partners or co-managers.

Anecdote: Documenting Day-to-Day Management for a Family-Owned Restaurant

An E-2 investor from Italy who co-owned a family restaurant in Chicago took on specific roles, including inventory management, supplier relations, and marketing. She documented her contributions through monthly reports and financial oversight records, which proved helpful during her renewal process.

Tip: If you're sharing management duties, make sure your roles are clearly differentiated. Regularly document your work and keep copies of emails, reports, and schedules that show your active involvement.

Staying Compliant Post-Approval: Monitoring Financials, Reporting, and Maintaining Active Involvement

Once your E-2 visa is approved, staying compliant means actively managing your business, keeping finances transparent, and ensuring that you're meeting visa requirements. Here's how to avoid post-approval compliance pitfalls and keep your visa status secure.

1. Tracking Financial Health and Reporting

USCIS wants to see that your business is financially viable, so maintaining clear financial records is essential. Tracking your income, expenses, and profits helps ensure you're meeting expectations and provides vital documentation for renewals.

Case Study: Tracking Financial Progress for a Landscaping Business

An E-2 investor from Japan who ran a landscaping business in Texas made it a habit to review his financials monthly, tracking profits, employee wages, and tax obligations. This proactive approach not only kept his business stable but also allowed him to present clear financial records for his renewal, which helped avoid potential issues.

Tip: Set up a monthly financial review to stay on top of income and expenses. This habit is not only good for business but also provides crucial documentation for USCIS during renewals.

2. Regularly Reviewing and Updating Business Plans

Your business plan isn't a one-and-done document—it's a tool to guide growth and document progress. Regularly updating it with new goals, strategies, and financial projections shows USCIS that you're committed to business development.

Anecdote: Updating the Business Plan for a Café Expansion

An E-2 investor from Argentina ran a popular café in Miami and decided to expand by opening a second location. She updated her business plan to reflect her expansion strategy, new employee hiring, and projected revenue increase. These updates showed USCIS her commitment to growth and made her renewal application stronger.

Tip: Revisit your business plan annually and make updates to reflect changes in your business strategy, market conditions, and goals. A well-maintained plan demonstrates to USCIS that your business is evolving and sustainable.

3. Documenting Active Involvement in Business Operations

Active involvement is a key E-2 requirement, so it's important to document your management role. USCIS will want to see that you're actively steering the business rather than acting as a passive investor. Monthly reports, meeting notes, and even emails showing decision-making can be useful evidence of your involvement.

Example: Monthly Reports for a Real Estate Firm

An E-2 investor from the UK who managed a real estate consulting firm in Los Angeles kept monthly reports detailing client acquisitions, property evaluations, and team meetings. When it came time for his renewal, these reports clearly showed his day-to-day involvement, which reinforced his role as an active manager.

Tip: Regularly document your contributions to business operations. You don't need to save every email, but keeping a record of key decisions, meetings, and strategies can go a long way in showing USCIS that you're actively involved.

4. Keeping up with Local and Federal Compliance Requirements

Aside from USCIS requirements, it's essential to stay on top of local and federal regulations, including tax laws, licensing requirements, and employee rights. Compliance with these laws ensures your business operates smoothly and avoids legal issues.

Anecdote: Navigating Local Regulations for a Boutique

An E-2 investor from Italy opened a boutique in New York and made sure to keep up with city regulations, including retail licensing and sales tax filing. This proactive approach not only kept her business in good standing but also reflected well on her during her visa renewal process.

Tip: Set reminders for compliance deadlines, such as tax filings and license renewals. Staying compliant with local regulations protects your business and supports your E-2 renewal case.

Bringing It All Together

The E-2 visa journey is filled with opportunities, but it also comes with responsibilities. By staying vigilant with your documentation, carefully managing partnerships, and actively participating in your business, you can avoid common pitfalls and keep your business and visa status secure.

Remember, attention to detail and proactive management can make all the difference. Whether it's double-checking documentation, maintaining your business plan, or actively overseeing daily operations, each step helps strengthen your E-2 case. With these strategies, you'll be well-equipped to avoid mistakes and keep your E-2 business thriving.

CHAPTER 14: SUCCESS STORIES AND CASE STUDIES

The E-2 visa journey is full of unique challenges and incredible rewards. For some, it means building a business from scratch in a new country, while for others, it's about turning a dream into reality with persistence and vision. Whether you're looking for inspiration, insights, or practical advice, learning from those who have successfully navigated the E-2 process can be invaluable.

In this chapter, we'll explore real-world examples of successful E-2 investors across different industries, discover lessons they learned along the way, and hear directly from experts who work closely with E-2 applicants. These stories showcase the power of resilience, adaptability, and a willingness to embrace the unknown.

Profiles of Successful E-2 Investors: Real-World Examples Across Industries

Let's dive into some success stories from E-2 investors in different fields. From food and hospitality to tech and retail, these stories show how diverse the E-2 journey can be.

1. Lucia's Italian Café: From Home-Cooked Meals to a Full-Service Restaurant

Lucia, an E-2 investor from Italy, turned her passion for Italian cooking into a thriving restaurant in Austin, Texas. Her journey began when she moved to the U.S. and started hosting small dinner parties, which became so popular that her friends encouraged her to open a restaurant. Her path to success was filled with challenges, including navigating local health regulations and sourcing authentic Italian ingredients.

After securing her E-2 visa, Lucia opened *Cucina di Lucia* with a small team. Her dedication to quality and authenticity attracted a loyal following, and the restaurant grew by word of mouth. Lucia reinvested in the business, expanding her menu and adding a small patio area. Her story exemplifies how passion and authenticity can resonate with American customers, creating a unique brand that stands out in a competitive market.

Tip: Lucia's success came from staying true to her vision. She focused on creating an authentic Italian experience rather than trying to fit into a "standard" American dining model. If you have a unique perspective, lean into it—it might just be your biggest asset.

2. Omar's Tech Start-Up: A Visionary Approach to Cybersecurity

Omar, an E-2 investor from Egypt, had a background in computer science and cybersecurity. He noticed a growing need for small and medium businesses to protect themselves from cyber threats, but many couldn't afford comprehensive security solutions. So, he launched a company in San Francisco that offers affordable cybersecurity packages tailored to smaller organizations.

Starting in a competitive market, Omar faced challenges like finding clients and building a reputation. To gain traction, he offered free consultations to local businesses, allowing them to understand their vulnerabilities and see the value of his services. This strategy worked, and soon, Omar's company became known as the go-to provider for affordable cybersecurity. Today, his firm employs a team of cybersecurity experts, and he's expanded his services to include cybersecurity training for small business owners.

Tip: Omar's strategy of offering consultations built trust and allowed him to connect personally with his clients. If your business is service-based, consider how a "preview" or trial offering can build credibility and create long-term client relationships.

3. Ayesha's Retail Boutique: Finding Success with Unique Offerings

Ayesha, an E-2 investor from India, moved to New York with a dream of opening a boutique that showcased the unique, hand-crafted jewelry of Indian artisans. After identifying a niche in the market, she opened *Kalyana*, a boutique in Brooklyn that offers one-of-a-kind jewelry pieces made from sustainable materials.

Her journey wasn't without hurdles—importing goods, managing shipping costs, and navigating U.S. retail laws were all new challenges. To attract customers, she collaborated with local fashion influencers and hosted jewelry-making workshops. This community-oriented approach created a loyal customer base and raised awareness for her brand. *Kalyana* is now a local favorite, and Ayesha plans to expand her brand online to reach a broader audience.

Tip: Ayesha's approach of building a community through workshops and collaborations with influencers was a major key to her success. Think about ways you can connect with your audience beyond traditional sales—sometimes, experiences and engagement can be your most effective marketing tools.

Lessons Learned from E-2 Journeys: Advice from Seasoned E-2 Holders on Navigating Challenges

Each E-2 investor has their unique journey, and with it, a wealth of lessons learned along the way. Here's some practical advice from E-2 holders who've been through the ups and downs of starting a business in the U.S.

1. Build a Network Early

Many E-2 investors find that one of their biggest assets is their network. Whether it's connecting with other business owners, mentors, or local community members, building a network early on can open doors to opportunities and provide invaluable support.

Example: Building Connections in the Community

Lucia, from *Cucina di Lucia*, joined a local business group shortly after opening her restaurant. This network connected her with local suppliers and even helped her find a more affordable restaurant space. She says that these connections made a significant difference, especially in her early days when every dollar and relationship counted.

Tip: Consider joining local business groups, industry associations, or online communities relevant to your field. Networking can lead to partnerships, advice, and even client referrals that might be harder to find on your own.

2. Adaptability is Key

In the U.S. market, customer expectations can shift quickly, and being able to adapt is essential. For example, Omar from the cybersecurity start-up learned that his clients valued on-demand support over scheduled consulting, so he adjusted his business model to offer more flexible options.

Example: Adjusting Services for Customer Satisfaction

Omar's willingness to listen to client feedback and make changes helped him retain clients and attract new ones. He discovered that adaptability wasn't just a strategy but a necessity for staying relevant in a fast-paced industry like tech.

Tip: Pay attention to feedback from clients and industry trends. Even small adjustments to your offerings or business model can make a big difference in customer satisfaction and long-term success.

3. Keep Documentation Organized

One of the recurring challenges for E-2 investors is managing paperwork. From the initial application to visa renewals, keeping records is essential. Ayesha from *Kalyana* boutique learned this the hard way when she struggled to compile employee records for her visa renewal.

Anecdote: Staying on Top of Documentation for Peace of Mind

After facing delays in her renewal application due to disorganized records, Ayesha implemented a system for tracking all business expenses, tax documents, and employee records. This not only made the renewal process smoother but also helped her track her business's financial health more effectively.

Tip: Regularly update and organize your documents. Cloud storage can be helpful, allowing you to easily access and compile records whenever they're needed.

Interviews with Experts: Insights from Immigration Lawyers, Business Advisors, and Successful E-2 Investors

To bring you additional perspectives, we spoke with experts who regularly work with E-2 investors. These insights shed light on some of the most important factors to consider as you embark on or continue your E-2 journey.

1. Advice from an Immigration Lawyer: Understanding Visa Requirements and Compliance

We spoke with Sarah Lopez, an immigration lawyer with over 15 years of experience helping E-2 investors. Her key advice? "Be thorough with documentation from day one, and always keep an eye on compliance. Many investors get so wrapped up in running the business that they forget to track their active involvement and job creation, both of which are crucial for renewals."

Sarah also emphasized the importance of planning for renewal early. "It's best to treat each renewal as if it's your first application—gather all your documentation, keep financials transparent, and show that you're still actively running the business. It's easier to prepare if you treat compliance as an ongoing process rather than a last-minute scramble."

Tip: Set regular reminders to update your documentation and track compliance. A little organization now can save you a lot of time and stress during renewal.

2. Insights from a Business Advisor: Growth Strategies for Small E-2 Businesses

Mark Davison, a business advisor specializing in small business growth, works frequently with E-2 investors. His advice focuses on growth strategies: "For E-2 businesses, growth doesn't always mean expanding locations or hiring a large team. It's often about smart, sustainable growth—adding services, diversifying offerings, and building brand loyalty."

He also noted that many E-2 investors overlook digital marketing. "A solid online presence can transform a small business," Mark explains. "Whether it's through social media, an e-commerce site, or even email marketing, digital channels can help you reach a larger audience without needing a big budget."

Tip: Think about growth in terms of reach and engagement, not just size. Digital marketing, local partnerships, and community involvement are all ways to grow sustainably.

3. Wisdom from a Seasoned E-2 Investor

Finally, we spoke with Tom O'Brien, an E-2 investor from the U.K. who has successfully renewed his visa multiple times for his consulting firm in Chicago. His biggest piece of advice is to "always be ready for the unexpected."

"When I started out, I thought I had everything under control, but the U.S. market was different from what I was used to," Tom recalls. "I quickly learned that adaptability and resilience were my best tools. Don't be afraid to pivot if something's not working—sometimes the U.S. customer base has different needs than you're used to."

Tip: Stay flexible and keep an open mind. Embracing new ideas and adjusting to the U.S. market can lead to growth and even unexpected opportunities.

Bringing It All Together

Every E-2 journey is unique, and hearing from those who've been through it provides valuable insights. Whether it's the adaptability of a tech start-up, the community connections of a restaurant, or the resourcefulness of a retail boutique, these stories showcase the resilience and determination that define successful E-2 investors.

As you navigate your own E-2 experience, remember that there's no single "right" way to succeed. What matters is that you stay focused, organized, and open to learning. With the right mindset and strategies, you can overcome challenges, make meaningful connections, and build a thriving business that stands the test of time.

This chapter provides real-world stories, expert insights, and actionable tips for E-2 investors. Let me know if you'd like additional detail on any section!

APPENDICES

Appendix A: List of E-2 Treaty Countries

The E-2 visa is available only to nationals from countries that have an investment treaty with the United States. Below is a list of treaty countries. If your country isn't listed, you may want to explore options such as acquiring citizenship from a treaty country.

E-2 Treaty Countries (As of [Year])

- **Europe**: Albania, Austria, Belgium, Denmark, France, Germany, Ireland, Italy, Netherlands, Norway, Spain, Switzerland, United Kingdom, and others.
- **Asia**: Japan, South Korea, Taiwan, Thailand, and others.
- **Latin America**: Argentina, Chile, Colombia, Costa Rica, Honduras, Mexico, Panama, and others.
- **Middle East & Africa**: Egypt, Israel, Jordan, Morocco, and others.
- **Oceania**: Australia, New Zealand.

Note: For a comprehensive and updated list of E-2 treaty countries, consult the official U.S. Department of State website.

Appendix B: Sample Business Plan and Document Templates

A solid business plan and well-organized documentation are essential for a successful E-2 visa application. Here, you'll find sample templates to guide you in crafting a business plan and organizing key documents. These templates can be customized to fit your specific business and meet E-2 requirements.

1. Sample Business Plan Outline

This business plan template is specifically designed to meet E-2 application standards. The structure includes sections for market research, revenue projections, and your role as an active manager, making it easy to create a comprehensive document that satisfies USCIS requirements.

- **Executive Summary**: Brief overview of the business, including mission, vision, and primary goals.
- **Business Description**: Detailed description of the business model, industry, and competitive landscape.
- **Market Analysis**: Data on target market, demographics, and key competitors.
- **Products or Services**: Description of your offerings and how they meet market needs.
- **Marketing and Sales Strategy**: Plan for attracting customers, including promotional strategies, pricing, and sales tactics.
- **Management and Staffing**: Explanation of the management structure, including your role and the roles of any key team members.
- **Financial Projections**: Three-year revenue and expense forecast, with assumptions and justifications.
- **Funding and Investment**: Summary of your investment, including the source and intended use of funds.

2. Proof of Funds Documentation Template

Creating a clear, traceable documentation of your funds is crucial. Here's a checklist template for organizing proof of funds:

- **Source of Funds**: Bank statements, tax returns, or property sale documents.
- **Transfer Documentation**: Wire transfer records showing funds transferred to a U.S. account.
- **Investment Breakdown**: Summary of initial

investment and how funds are allocated within the business.

3. Sample Employee Record Template

This template helps you document employee information, which is especially helpful when meeting job creation requirements:

- **Employee Name**
- **Job Title and Role**
- **Hire Date**
- **Wages and Benefits**
- **Hours Worked per Week**

Keeping records in this format allows you to easily compile information when demonstrating your business's economic impact.

Final Thoughts on the E-2 Journey

Establishing your business in the U.S. on an E-2 visa is a unique journey filled with opportunities and challenges. Whether you're crafting your business plan, applying for renewal, or planning for long-term growth, the resources in these appendices are designed to support you every step of the way. Use these tools, templates, and professional resources to simplify the process and set yourself up for lasting success in the U.S. market.

www.ingramcontent.com/pod-product-compliance
Lightning Source LLC
Chambersburg PA
CBHW070143230526
45471CB00002B/494